# A Decade Driving the Dixie Highway

## Exploring the USA's first highway system

DENNY GIBSON

ISBN: 0692516964
ISBN-13: 978-0692516966

# ACKNOWLEDGMENTS

Thanks to Robert V. Droz for the US-Highways website
(http://us-highways.com) and the directions that formed the basis of many of
my Dixie Highway travels. A huge amount of thanks goes to Russell S. Rein and
Mike Curtis for helping me improve my routes on many occasions as well as for
looking this book over and heading off some errors. Extra thanks to Mike for
taking the time to clarify many of the Dixie Highway Association's route
designations and to locate those Robert E. Lee markers. I very much appreciate
the assistance that both Pat Bremer and Jim Grey provided in finding the DH in
Indiana. Pat also helped with some Kentucky bits and Jim's the guy that got me
headed the right way out of South Bend back in 2008. Mike Buettner's research
was quite helpful in tracing the route in Ohio. Routing and other assistance also
came from the Dixie Highway Facebook group
(http://www.facebook.com/groups/DixieHwy/).

Brian Butko's encouragement and insightful advice were truly invaluable and I
am seriously grateful to Laurel Kane for her sensible and skillful proofreading.
Thanks to Christopher Miller and the Berea College Loyal Jones Appalachian
Center in Berea, Kentucky, for allowing me to photograph the Dixie Highway
"cotton bale" sign for this book's cover.

# Contents

**The Dixie Highway as driven**

# 1 THERE IT IS

The Dixie Highway was the first historic road I ever encountered. At the time, though, I didn't even know what a historic road was let alone that the Dixie Highway was one. I first recall seeing a Dixie Drive sign on a childhood visit to see relatives in Dayton, Ohio, and thinking it an odd name for a street in a town so far north but, over time, it became just another street name. Sightings continued and probably increased when I started driving and made the occasional trip to Dayton myself. After moving to Cincinnati in the mid-1960s, I spotted even more signs bearing the word Dixie including some expressway exit signs across the river in Kentucky.

Somewhere along the way I learned that many of these signs identified pieces of the same road and that that road connected "up north" with "down south" but it didn't mean much to me. Old roads of any sort didn't mean much to me then. I drove to Miami Beach in 1968 and I have to believe the trip involved a little Dixie Highway but I probably didn't notice and I certainly don't remember. I do recall driving winding two-lane and, though my country boy background made me feel more comfortable there than on the interstate, that wasn't the reason. The reason was simply that, in 1968, many gaps remained to be filled in the modern interstate highway system. It seems all but certain that I got through some of those gaps on former Dixie Highway roadway. If only I'd realized. If only I'd cared.

Thirty years later, in 1999, my attraction to old roads was nudged with a trip on Route 66. In 2001, I took a trip that should have brought the Dixie Highway front and center but it didn't. My great-grandparents had driven to Florida in 1920 in a Ford Model T and I attempted to retrace their path. By then I was becoming aware of the named auto trails that preceded the system of Numbered US Highways but I did not fully appreciate them or know many details.

I did know that both the Dixie Highway and my great-grandparents passed through Cincinnati on their way to Miami so I naturally wondered if they traveled together. I compared my crude and preliminary plot of their route with my even cruder and woefully incomplete picture of the Dixie Highway. At the time, I don't believe I really comprehended that the Dixie Highway was itself a highway system. I thought it was just another point A to point B route. It did not help things at all that I more or less equated the Dixie Highway with US 25.

Granddad and Granny departed Cincinnati on a path that I thought might have been the Dixie Highway but at Lexington they turned to the west and away from the DH as I believed it to be. Nothing I had from my great-grandparents concerning their trip mentioned the Dixie Highway by name and I took that Lexington turn as proof that it was not a part of their travel plans at all. If I knew then what I know now, I might have seen that what they did was merely move from the DH East Mainline to the DH West Mainline on their own "connector". Their 1920 path certainly did not precisely follow the Dixie Highway but the main problem with my thinking was my lack of knowledge of the Dixie and just how complex it was. I now believe that much of the driving I did in 2001 not only followed Granddad's tire tracks but followed the Dixie Highway, too.

I know I followed more Dixie Highway during the next three years but sometimes didn't realize it and other times did not think it significant. I had started documenting my trips on a website with that 1999 Route 66 outing but it wasn't until 2004 and the twentieth trip that I mentioned the Dixie Highway in my online journal.

The occasion was an event at the National Corvette Museum in Bowling Green, Kentucky. We were staying at the 1937 Wigwam Village #2 in Cave City and driving to and from the museum on

US 31W. I didn't mention the Dixie Highway by name when I posted my first ever photos of the tepee shaped accommodations and the closed Horseshoe Camp Cabins we passed along the way but I clearly knew these places were on the historic road. The road that passes Wigwam Village is signed Dixie Highway and I did use the name when posting pictures of the ruins of Bell's Tavern in nearby Park City. It is almost certain that I had passed both Wigwam Village and Horseshoe Camp on that 2001 trip but I mentioned neither in my journal.

**Horse Shoe Camp Motel near Bowling Green, KY (Apr 23, 2004)**

The 2004 photo of the 1930s era Horse Shoe Camp Motel was taken one day before my first recognition of the Dixie Highway in an online trip report. I did not make plans to drive the entire Dixie Highway on that trip but the seeds were certainly planted. The heyday of the Horse Shoe Camp Motel had trailed that of the Dixie but only by a few years. The stone cabins and rusted sign were physical reminders that there is as much history and as many interesting stories beside what was once the Dixie Highway as beside any of America's historic highways. I would travel this section and photograph this motel several more times before reaching some other sections of the Dixie Highway for the first time.

# 2 HOW IT GOT THERE

Carl Fisher, the idea man behind the Indianapolis Speedway and the Lincoln Highway is also credited with being the idea man behind the Dixie Highway and the developer of Miami Beach. These last two are not exactly unconnected. It would not, in fact, be entirely wrong to suggest that the Dixie Highway came to be so Carl Fisher could sell Florida real estate. Fisher was not, of course, the first person to think about a road connecting north and south. Hatching good ideas is important. Sharing them with the right people even more so. Carl Fisher was pretty good at both.

Among those with whom Fisher shared his idea were fellow Indianans Samuel Ralston and William S. Gilbreath. Ralston was Indiana's governor and Gilbreath was secretary of the Hoosier Motor Club. With support from Ralston, Gilbreath took advantage of the attention aimed at the 1914 American Road Congress meeting in Atlanta to publicize the idea.

The concept, when Fisher first mentioned it to an *Indianapolis News* reporter, was to "build a great highway from Indianapolis to Miami, Florida". He offered up the name "Hoosier Land-to-Dixie Highway". By the time of that Atlanta meeting, in November 1914, it seems Chicago had become the northern terminus and "Cotton Belt Route" had become the popular name. Chicago and Miami would be almost alone in retaining their roles while nearly every other aspect of the "great highway" changed – and changed quickly – around them. I am not foolish enough to attempt a detailed play-by-play of those early days. I'll limit myself to some highlights.

Obviously the name changed. Within weeks , the name "Dixie Highway" was in common use. It became official on April 3, 1915, when the Dixie Highway Association was formed in Chattanooga, Tennessee. The name came from a vision for the highway to be a great aid in uniting north and south. In an article reporting on the Association's formation, the *New York Times* described the road as "a monument to celebrate the half century of peace within the Union" and even called it "The Dixie Peaceway".

It should be no surprise that Illinois, Indiana, Kentucky, Tennessee, Georgia, and Florida were represented at the meeting. Those are all states crossed by a straight line between Chicago and Miami. But Ohio was also present indicating that plans were already in motion to somehow get that state on the route.

There was good reason for Ohio to be involved. It had a very active highway department with considerable paved roadway. Ohioans pushed for their state to be included on the route and it was. It seems that even before the April meeting, the organizers decided that, rather than pick one of the two possible routes through Kentucky, they would use both. The highway would split at Indianapolis with one branch heading south through Louisville while the other followed the National Old Trails Road east to Dayton, Ohio, then turned south to pass through Cincinnati and Lexington. With that first split, the Dixie Highway ceased being a common point-to-point route and started to become a highway system.

States were represented from the top at that April organizational meeting. It was Indiana's Governor Ralston who called the conference and he, along with the governors of four of the other states, attended and even the two states whose governors were not there, Florida and Ohio, had representatives personally appointed by their governors. Having state governments participate in the association was key to its success. The meeting was not without its drama and confrontations but in the end it established that all decisions, particularly routing decisions, would be made by a board of directors with the governor of each state appointing two members.

June 20, 1916

By the time a second meeting was held in Chattanooga in May, Michigan had made a case for being included and, at the meeting's conclusion, more drama notwithstanding, it was. With Michigan now officially a Dixie Highway state, a second northern terminus was designated at Mackinaw City, Michigan, and any pretense of this being a simple A to B highway vanished. The map from June of 1916, when the Dixie Highway Association was just over a year old, shows what amounts to two mainlines with the exception of the area between Chattanooga, Tennessee, and Macon, Georgia. Auxiliary routes abound.

On June 18, 1918, North and South Carolina were admitted to the DHA and plans made for a route between Knoxville, Tennessee, and Waynesboro, Georgia. Two distinct paths now existed over the highway's entire length. A tourist could drive the Dixie Highway all the way from Chicago to Miami (or at least Melbourne or West Palm Beach) without ever using any of the Dixie Highway driven by another tourist coming from Mackinaw City.

The November 1, 1923, map is the last one showing the entire system that was issued by the DHA before it disbanded in 1927. The East Mainline's northern terminus has moved to Sault Sainte Marie and various auxiliary routes have come or gone. Curiously, it shows the southernmost part of the West Mainline utilizing the Tamiami Trail and eliminates other routes across southern Florida. Since the Tamiami Trail did not open until 1928, the map can certainly be considered somewhat forward looking.

OFFICIAL MAP
OF THE
DIXIE HIGHWAY
ISSUED BY
DIXIE HIGHWAY ASSOCIATION
CHATTANOOGA, TENN.
NOVEMBER 1ST, 1923.

November 1, 1923

# 3 WHAT IT IS

Improvements and realignments make the precise route of just about any road more than a few yards long and twenty-four hours old open to debate. That is true for simple point A to point B roads and overwhelmingly true for a road that goes from points C and S to point M and hits most of the rest of the alphabet on the way. Even talking about the Dixie Highway's various parts is problematic.

Imagine a person coming upon that final 1923 Dixie Highway Association map with no prior knowledge of the road or its history. A reasonable interpretation of the map might be that it shows a highway starting at Sault Sainte Marie, splitting at Mackinaw City, and following two primary routes to Miami. In a few places, two alternate paths are shown for getting between two points and there are some paths that connect one of the primary routes with the other. Chicago is connected via the solitary feeder route.

That might be a reasonable interpretation  but it is not quite the one that the map's makers had in mind. Unlike the imaginary person in the preceding paragraph, the 1923 mappers were quite knowledgeable of the highway's history and couldn't ignore it – at least sometimes. The Dixie Highway Association certainly ignored something when it stopped referring to Chicago as the northern terminus of the Western Division and started calling Sault Sainte Marie the northern terminus of the Dixie Highway rather than of just the Eastern Division. This seems to have happened around 1919.

More or less from the beginning, the word "division" was used by the DHA to identify sections of the highway. At first there was an Eastern Division and Western Division. A third division was added in 1918. The route involved was one connecting Knoxville, Tennessee, and Waynesboro, Georgia. These cities were already connected by the Eastern Division but, for a significant part of the way, it shared the road with the Western Division. If that imaginary person with no prior knowledge of the DH was told about the two divisions and that the Knoxville-Waynesboro route was a late addition, they might assume that the Eastern Division was moved to incorporate the new route and leave the Western Division alone. But what actually happened was that the addition was given the name Carolina Division and the Eastern and Western Divisions continued to share roadway between Chattanooga and Atlanta.

My earliest exposure to the structure of the Dixie Highway came from a website that identified each bit of DH as mainline, connector, or loop. I don't know whether or not Robert V. Droz, the creator of us-highways.com, invented the classifications but they made sense to me and, with one exception, would probably make sense to our imaginary map discoverer. The exception is that Droz, very much aware of Dixie Highway history, kept Chicago as a primary route terminus. His two *mainlines* are the direct routes from the northern termini (Chicago and Sault Sainte Marie) to Miami, *connectors* have an endpoint on each of the two mainlines, and *loops* have both endpoints on the same mainline. The mainlines are identified as east (Sault Sainte Marie) and west (Chicago) while connectors are typically identified by the region they are in and loops by the name of a city they pass through.

If I were setting out today to clinch the Dixie Highway, I might very well target only the alignments included in that 1923 map. There are certainly real and official pieces of Dixie Highway that are not on that map but it is a complete and coherent representation of the DHA's view of its highway.

As it was, the only catalog, not to mention driving instructions, I initially had available was the us-highways.com website. It contains both more and less than the final DHA map.

Droz identified ten connectors and five loops. Two of those loops do not appear on any Dixie Highway Association map that I have seen. On the other hand, there are two other loops on the last full DHA map that Droz does not include. In case that's not confusing enough, there is at least one loop that carries Dixie Highway signs and is generally accepted as part of the DH that does not appear on either the DHA maps or Droz's list. I included "all the above" in my driving agenda.

The Dixie Highway components Droz identifies are:

West Mainline – Chicago to Miami
East Mainline – Sault Sainte Marie to Miami
Northern Connector – Mackinaw City, MI, to Indianapolis, IN
Midwestern Connector – Indianapolis, IN, to Dayton, OH
Tennessee Connector – Knoxville, TN, to Chattanooga, TN
Georgia Connector – Atlanta, GA, to Waynesboro, GA
Southern Connector – Macon, GA, to Jacksonville, FL
North Florida Connector – Tallahassee, FL, to Jacksonville, FL
East Florida Connector – Hastings, FL, to Orlando, FL
Central Florida Connector – Kissimmee, FL, to Melborne, FL
Scenic Highlands Connector – Haines City, FL, to Okeechobee, FL
South Florida Connector – Arcadia, FL, to West Palm Beach, FL
Port Huron Loop – Bay City, MI, to Detroit, MI
Flint Bypass Loop – Bay City, MI, to Pontiac, MI
Cumberland Gap Loop – Corbin, KY, to Newport, TN
Rome Loop – Chattanooga, TN, to Cartersville, GA
Tampa-Saint Petersburg Loop – Ocala, FL, to Haines City, FL

Of these, neither the Flint Bypass Loop nor the Tampa-Saint Petersburg Loop are shown on Dixie Highway Association maps. I've identified the three loops not on the Droz list as:

Holland Loop – Ferrysburg, MI, to Niles, MI
Falmouth Loop – Covington, KY, to Lexington, KY
Monroe Loop – Franklin, OH, to Cincinnati, OH

Boosters in Saint Petersburg were given temporary authorization to develop a route through their city with final inclusion dependent on meeting certain deadlines for improving it. Minutes of DHA meetings indicate that, after the deadlines were extended and still not met, all authorization was about to be revoked but there is no record of an actual vote or revocation. A somewhat similar situation existed with the Falmouth Loop although it at least made it to the DHA map. It was added as an alternate route between Cincinnati and Lexington with plans to eventually decide on just one of the two routes as permanent. There is no record of that decision ever being made, either.

The Monroe Loop may have had no DHA involvement at all. When the Numbered US Highways were established in 1926, most of the Dixie Highway in Ohio became US 25. It seems reasonable to believe that, when the US route was moved after a few years, the Dixie Highway tagged along even though it didn't exactly exist anymore. The Flint Bypass Loop may be another situation where local patterns created a real but unofficial path for the DH. Of the five "special" loops, only the Holland Loop is a straight forward last minute official addition to the Dixie Highway.

No one should consider the routes I plotted and followed as complete or correct. I certainly don't. Not only did the highway evolve, so too did my understanding of it. My knowledge of the Dixie Highway changed a whole bunch from that first documented touch in 2004 through deciding to attempt a clinch to declaring it done. Note that, even though I use the word "clinch", I make no claim to have driven every inch of roadway that was ever part of the Dixie Highway. I do, however, think I've driven something that closely approximates all of it that was officially recognized by the Dixie Highway Association – and then some.

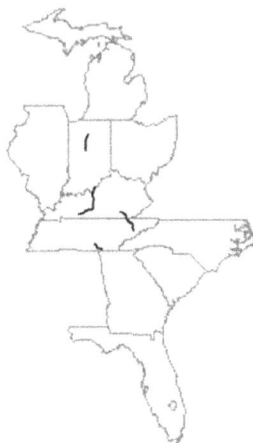

# 4 BITS AND PIECES

*A Decade Driving the Dixie Highway* isn't really accurate, you know. I've mentioned seeing Dixie Highway related signs as a child in the 1950s. Maybe I could have called this book *A Lifetime Driving the Dixie Highway* if those early sightings had made a bigger impression or I followed up on them sooner. Instead, I've decided to peg the beginning of my Dixie Highway quest to the Horse Shoe Camp Motel stop on April 23, 2004. I finished driving my unofficial version of the Dixie Highway on July 22, 2015 when I reached the highway's original start point in Chicago. *Eleven Years, Two Months, and Twenty-Nine Days Driving the Dixie Highway* would have been wonderfully precise but seems overly long and hard to remember. So "decade" it is -- fairly short, slightly alliterative, easy to remember, and close enough.

I may have known I was on the Dixie Highway when I pulled over by the abandoned motel in 2004 and I may have even told the world, via the internet, one day later but I didn't immediately set out to drive the whole thing nor did I even start tracking what I did drive. 2009 would be nearly over before I even suggested that I might try to drive the entire Dixie Highway and it was two more years before I checked and shared my progress. I did, however, note several Dixie Highway contacts in the meantime.

Just a couple of months after that first Horse Shoe Camp visit, I attended a Route 66 festival in Tulsa, Oklahoma, and used US 60 to get me most of the way home. As it nears Louisville, Kentucky, US 60 joins up with US 31W and both routes enter the city along the path once used by the Dixie Highway. I noted this in my online journal but didn't document any Dixie Highway features. Near Cincinnati, I drove a little more Dixie Highway but did not bother to identify it. It is the West Mainline that runs through Louisville and the East Mainline that runs through Cincinnati so you could say that I used I-71 as a Dixie Highway connector.

In November my job took me to Georgia and I knowingly drove some Dixie Highway coming home although I didn't really plan it or make any effort to tightly follow the old route. The work assignment was in Royston which is Ty Cobb's home town and kind of cool in its own right. When I left, I took US 29 through Athens, then, after enduring mile-wide expressways through Atlanta, moved onto US 41 which I followed to Nashville, Tennessee.

Between Cassville, Georgia, and Nashville, US 41 mostly follows the route of the Dixie Highway. A significant exception is that, between the Tennessee towns of Monteagle and Murfreesboro, it is US 41A rather than 41 that follows the former Dixie Highway. That means I missed about 75 miles of the DH on this pass.

I returned to Georgia on business in December and I again got in a little Dixie Highway. In fact, I was on the Dixie both going and coming. The going bit wasn't much.

The front ends of business trips rarely had much slack time and this was no exception. I couldn't really leave the expressway to leisurely drive along the Dixie Highway in its guise of US 25W but I did slip off of it to see a roadside attraction I'd recently learned of. Like the Horse Shoe Camp Motel I first saw in April, I would visit the airplane shaped service station in Powell, Tennessee, several more times before I finished driving the full Dixie Highway. On this first visit I dashed from the nearest I-75 exit and up maybe half a mile of US 25W to grab some photos.

**Nickle Brothers service station, Powell, TN (Dec 8, 2004)**

A group had recently formed to tackle saving the 1930 structure and a banner asking for donations hung on the side of the plane. I made sure I included the address when I photographed the banner then jumped back in the car and scurried along to my job.

Travel following a job related visit usually allowed for a little flexibility and, as I had in November, I looked for an interesting path home. The interesting path I chose included a stop at Babyland General Hospital (where Cabbage Patch Kids come from) in Cleveland, Georgia, and a run of the Tail of the Dragon. Babyland was interesting but I confess to finding it just a little creepy and driving a Pontiac Vibe uphill in light rain on the wiggling mountain road that motorcyclists race downhill on wasn't all that thrilling either. I did, however, eventually reach Newport, Tennessee, and what I believed to be the south end of the Dixie Highway's Cumberland Loop. In reality, the loop had run directly between Tazewell and Knoxville and had never included Newport.

**Old US 25E near Tazewell, TN (Dec 11, 2004)**

I had an enjoyable, though DH-less, drive to Tazewell then found a short stretch of Old Highway 25E, and possibly old Dixie Highway, just north of town. Cumberland Gap was officially removed from the Dixie Highway in 1918 but continued to be used as an "alternate" until the more direct route through La Follette was completed. The road through Cumberland Gap, which had earned the nickname "Massacre Mountain", was eliminated by a pair of tunnels that opened in 1996 and now carry US 25E under the park. Not only was the road bypassed, the asphalt has been removed as part of a plan to restore the area to its eighteenth century appearance.

**US 25W near Duff, TN (Nov 23, 2006)**

I noted touching the Dixie Highway again in April 2005 when I drove the Lincoln Highway across Ohio including the half mile or so the Dixie and Lincoln share in Beaverdam. In November of 2006, expressway boredom prompted me to make an impromptu drive of roughly thirty miles of Dixie Highway at the north edge of Tennessee. The winding two-lane US 25 between Jellico and Caryville is rather scenic as it, the river, and the railroad are often side by side.

I stayed with US 25 as it rejoined then exited I-75. This took me through Clinton and Cridersville and past the Powell Airplane. The old service station had received a little attention in the two years since I first saw it but I suspected that the deterioration had only been slowed and was not yet stopped.

**Nickle Brothers service station, Powell, TN (Nov 23, 2006)**

Though I knew the Powell Airplane was on the Dixie Highway and both of my visits were deliberate, they could hardly be called planned Dixie Highway excursions. Even the 2006 drive, which departed the expressway several miles north of the plane, did not seek out old Dixie alignments but merely followed the current US 25. It would be the next spring before I made any real effort to follow a piece of the old highway.

In April 2007, a small group of road fans gathered in Cave City, Kentucky, specifically to drive some historic roadway. The group, with members from Illinois, Indiana, Missouri, Ohio, and Tennessee, spent two nights at Wigwam Village #2. On the day in between, we drove the Dixie Highway north to Elizabethtown then, after cutting over to Bardstown on US 62, drove the Jackson Highway south to a point due east of Cave City before closing the circle back at the Wigwams. In this area, the Dixie is associated with US 31W and the Jackson with US 31E but we didn't limit ourselves to the US routes and tried to cover some segments of the named trails that current versions of the US routes sidestepped. We started with the narrow stretch of Dixie Highway that passes behind Wigwam Village #2.

**Wigwam Village, Cave City, KY (Apr 27, 2007)**

**Old Dixie Highway north of Cave City, KY (Mar 18, 2007)**

A little more than a year later, over the 2008 Memorial Day weekend, I made a rather unorganized trip to northern Indiana. The second day turned out to be a car museum marathon as I took in the

Auburn Cord Duesenberg Automobile Museum in Auburn, Hostetler's Hudsons in Shipshewana, and the Studebaker Museum in South Bend. With some online help from friends, I managed to find a little bit of the Dixie Highway on the third day as I traveled from South Bend to Indianapolis. Part of that little bit took me through Logansport and past Whitehouse No. 1.

**Whitehouse No. 1, Logansport, IN (May 26, 2008)**

Until it closed for the last time in August of 2014, Whitehouse No. 1 opened at 4:00 AM and closed no later than 1:00 PM. It was not open that first time I saw it in 2008 nor any of the other times I passed by. I regret that very much.

That Memorial Day weekend was the last time I stumbled onto the Dixie Highway unexpectedly or without some semblance of a plan.

# 5 FOR REAL AT LAST

No explanation exists for why it took me so long to get serious about the Dixie Highway. It's possible, I suppose, that part of the reason is that you often overlook things in your own backyard and that's where, to some degree, the Dixie was. From sign spotting in the 1950s through driving on streets with Dixie in their name in the 1960s and '70s to brief encounters as my attraction to old roads revealed itself, the Dixie Highway never quite caught my attention. When I realized that posting trip journals online was going to engage me beyond that first trip on Route 66, I gave the website a little structure that included a "Just Seeds" section that identified roads I hoped to drive someday. Early entries were the National Road, the Lincoln Highway, and US 22, which have all been completed, and US 50, which still awaits. When the list got very short, I added the Yellowstone Trail but the Dixie Highway never made it.

Sometime in 2008 I woke up. I didn't put the Dixie on the "Just Seeds" list but I did acknowledge that it had caught my attention. I made the DH part of trips over both Thanksgiving and Christmas and I didn't do it by accidentally bumping in to it or following some US route that had replaced it and only approximated the old route. For Thanksgiving I followed the Dixie Highway East Mainline to Asheville, North Carolina, and for Christmas I would head even further south to reach the southern terminus.

**John A. Roebling Bridge (Nov 27, 2008)**

The Dixie Highway crossed the Ohio River on the John A. Roebling Bridge throughout its entire existence and that's how I intended to begin my first "formal" Dixie Highway outing. It didn't happen. My departure coincided with the running of Cincinnati's Thanksgiving Day Race and, although the runners did not actually cross the bridge on that day, other street closings and temporary routings meant it was open only for northbound traffic. I crossed on another bridge then drove to the north end of the Roebling just to say I did and to get a picture. The bridge was just four days shy of the 142$^{nd}$ anniversary of its opening.

After another crossing on a substitute bridge, I picked up the DH at the Roebling's south end. I doubt my understanding of the Dixie's path through Covington, Kentucky, was perfect and I'm sure my following of it was not. Construction and one way streets having nothing to do with the foot race made sure of that. But I knew I was on the right course when I drove past the always open Anchor Grill and on out of town on US 25. Had there been any doubt, it would have been erased by the name on the front of the 1925 Water Works building at roadside.

**1925 Dixie Highway Water Company, Covington, KY (Nov 27, 2008)**

When the United States Numbered Highways System was established in 1926, US 25 took over the route of the Dixie Highway between Port Huron, Michigan, and North Augusta, South Carolina. In 1974, the route was decommissioned north of the Ohio River but continues to exist to the south In fact, it was extended southward on three occasions until its southern terminus reached Brunswick, Georgia, where it remains today. US 25 and the path of the Dixie Highway continue to be more or less an item until the DH turns eastward at Waynesboro, Georgia. That means that my entire run from Covington, Kentucky, to Asheville North Carolina, was on or beside US 25.

In and around built up areas like Covington and Lexington, US 25 is the unappealing four-or-more-lane road you would expect but an awful lot of the route through Kentucky is well maintained modern two-lane and fairly scenic. There are a few bypassed sections of older and narrower alignments but these also seemed to be well maintained. The road goes through quite a few small towns which add interest to the drive as well.

One place where US 25 and the Dixie Highway no longer match is just south of Berea, Kentucky. Here the US route was moved in 1927 to avoid the hills and twists of what is now called Scaffold Cane Road. While the Dixie Highway was routed over the road, a stone was placed at the boundary between Madison and Rockcastle counties that did more than just name the counties. The words "DIXIE HIGHWAY" are carved above the county names and distances to two nearby towns are carved below. Richmond lies 8 ½ miles north and Mt. Vernon is 14 miles south.

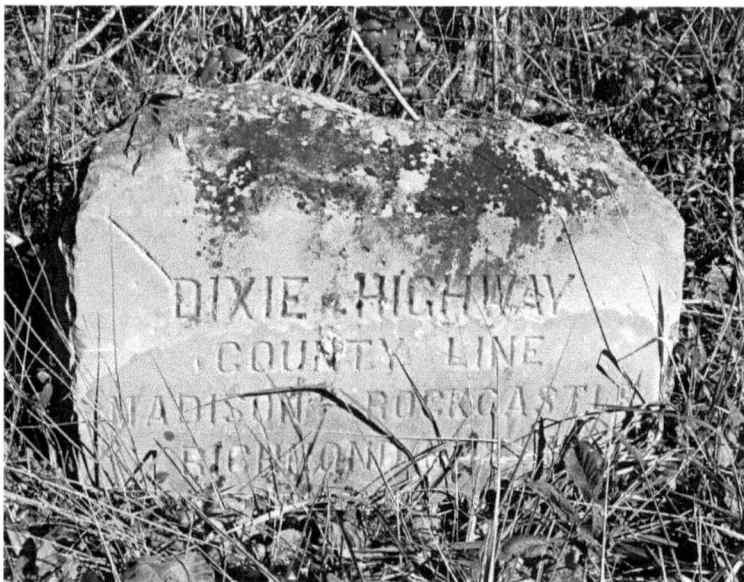

**Boundary of Madison and Rockcastle Counties, KY (Nov 27, 2008)**

At Corbin, US 25 splits into 25E and 25W which were both Dixie Highway. US 25W follows the path of East Mainline while 25E follows the Cumberland Gap Loop. I stayed with 25W and the Mainline.

At the Tennessee border I simply drove straight ahead to enjoy the scenic section I had spontaneously bolted to from I-75 two years before. I essentially repeated that drive to the north edge of Knoxville where I stopped for the night. I actually drove by the Powell Airplane before bedding down but there was no light for photographs and I intended to backtrack a little in the morning, anyway.

**Hoskins Drug Store, Clinton, TN (Nov 28, 2008)**

There were several reasons for the morning backtrack with the first being breakfast at Hoskins Drug Store. Hoskins started in downtown Clinton in 1930 and moved to this location on US 25W in 1947. The "restaurant" sign is justified by a genuine soda fountain serving breakfast and lunch. I entered and took a seat at the counter where a wonderful lady named Barbara promptly took my order. I glanced at the menu and ordered bacon and eggs. Just bacon and eggs. And coffee.

Barbara and I were the only ones in the store and things went silent for a moment before she asked, "No biscuits and gravy?"

It wasn't exactly accusing but it was close. Incredulous might be a better description. I don't always pick up on these things but I did that day. It was pretty clear that anyone not starting their day with gravy would almost certainly be looked at with suspicion in Clinton. I corrected my order immediately.

The second reason for backtracking was to stop by the Ciderville Music Store when it was open and the third was to drive some bypassed sections of concrete Old Clinton Pike that had once also been Dixie Highway. I had stopped by the store once before when it was closed but had seen and heard enough about it to know that I wanted to get inside. It is filled with guitars, banjos, mandolins, and the like and I understand that folks can frequently be heard playing some of them. I think I was just a little too early for that.

**Nickle Brothers service station, Powell, TN (Nov 28, 2008)**

The fourth reason for the backtrack was to make my third stop at the Powell Airplane. Things were definitely looking up with no more gaping holes and a tail that could stand on its own.

The Dixie heads almost due east out of Knoxville then angles slightly south to work its way across Douglas Lake and into the Cherokee National Forest. Halfway through the Forest, it enters North Carolina. A few miles beyond Hot Springs, while still within the National Forest, it turns southward toward Asheville. It's a rather scenic drive with the French Broad River and the Norfolk Southern railroad frequently in view. About halfway between Hot Springs and Asheville, the town of Marshall is squeezed into a narrow valley and the river, railroad, and highway enter the town side-by-side. The town, anchored by the Madison County Courthouse, looked to be worth a stop.

**Robert E. Lee and Dixie Highway marker in Marshall, NC (Nov 28, 2008)**

I parked the car for a closer look and read some of the markers standing in front of the courthouse. I was surprised to see the words "Dixie Highway" on one. Above them was the name Robert E. Lee and an image of the confederate general on horseback. The marker had been placed by the United Daughters of the Confederacy "in loving memory" of Lee and "to mark the route of the Dixie Highway". I would later learn that I had passed a couple of similar markers earlier in the day without seeing them and that there were others. Ten are known to exist and I would drive by several more without seeing them, either.

**Entrance to Biltmore Estate, Asheville, NC (Nov 28, 2008)**

Visiting the Biltmore Estate in Asheville was the justification for this trip and the trip's Dixie Highway portion ended pretty much at the estate's ready-for-Christmas entrance. Built at the end of the nineteenth century, the mansion was occupied and active when the Dixie Highway appeared at the gate and I wonder if George Washington Vanderbilt II ever hung out around the roadside to chat with tourists rattling by in their Model Ts.

This chapter began with a map and subsequent chapters will, too. Each shows the portion of Dixie Highway about to be covered.

# 6 THE SOUTHERNEST

Christmas break gave me another chance to hit the road and I again had the Dixie Highway on the agenda. The trip was focused on getting a little Key West weather into my life and spending Christmas Eve near where my great-grandparents did in 1920 but checking out some DH was only slightly less important. I've taken to calling my late December road trips Christmas Escape Runs. Usually that's about 50% joke. In 2008, "escape" was exactly the right word.

I left work mid-afternoon two days before Christmas and pulled into near gridlock. I made it home, grabbed my duffle, then spent nearly twenty minutes covering the half-mile to the expressway. It seemed the approaching storm had Christmas last-minute-shoppers and next-to-last-minute-shoppers out at the same time with the milk-and-bread crowd thrown in, too. It wasn't pretty.

I made it through Cincinnati ahead of the freezing temperatures but they soon caught up with me. In Kentucky, ice formed in the corners of the windshield and traffic slowed to a crawl. More than once, northbound traffic slowed to a stop. Cincinnati radio let me know that, behind me, accidents were "too numerous to count". But escape I did and at the end of the day I was warm and dry in Tampa.

I had headed to Tampa, or more specifically the Alafia River, because that's where my great-grandparents spent Christmas Eve in

1920 and it seemed like doing the same eighty-eight years later might be cool. Sitting on the river's south bank, Gibsonton, a winter home for circus people, promised to be a nice bonus.

Gibsonton, in particular the Showtown Restaurant and Lounge, was interesting but there wasn't much of 1920 left around the place. I spent Christmas Eve there and stopped by Showtown on Christmas morning for breakfast then I headed on south. South meant the Tamiami Trail.

**Tamiami Trail/US 41 in South Venice, FL (Dec 25, 2008)**

Taking its name from the cities it connected, Tampa and Miami, the Tamiami Trail officially opened on April 25, 1928. The Dixie Highway Association took up the Trail long before that. Construction began in 1915 and it was on a map that the Association published before the end of the decade. Not surprisingly, the Trail was also on the Association's final full system map (chapter 2). Surprisingly, the road between Arcadia and West Palm Beach was not. That map was published the same year, 1923, that the first test caravan spent three weeks traveling the 143 miles from Fort Myers to Miami. Considering this and the more than four years that would pass before the opening ceremony, it seems likely that the Arcadia-West Palm Beach route would, in practice, continue to comprise the southern end of the Dixie Highway West Mainline for awhile longer regardless of what the map said.

When I reached the Tamiami Trail, a bit more than eight decades after that official opening, it was in fine shape. It was not, however, the Dixie Highway. I had begun following the Trail at its beginning in Tampa so was already on it when I left the Showtown. The Dixie joined at Punta Gorda. Building this section was not very tough. In fact, no part of the north-south Tamiami Trail presented major road building challenges. Tampa to Naples was the easy part. It was the east-west section across the Everglades that took thirteen years, eight million dollars, and several lives.

**Alligator in Big Cypress National Preserve (Dec 26, 2008)**

Although I'm sure they are there, I spotted no alligators along the road. What I did see was lots of birds. About thirty miles east of Naples, the Big Cypress National Preserve provides a more reliable – and safer – way to see 'gators and it has plenty of birds, too.

**Miccosukee Indian Village (Dec 26, 2008)**

When the Everglades section of I-75 (a.k.a. Alligator Alley) opened in 1968 it took a lot of tourists and the enterprising folk who trap them away from the Tamiami Trail but plenty of both remain. I checked out Miccosukee Indian Village but skipped a planned stop at Coopertown, where the airboat was invented, because of the huge crowd. Road stubs signed Old Tamiami Trail run east and west from Miccosukee Indian Village but they are covered with recent vintage asphalt and just as straight and level as the current Trail. In the picture, the people heading toward the Village are walking across Old Tamiami Trail.

In Miami, I put the Dixie Highway on hold for a day. The DH West Mainline and the Tamiami Trail, being one and the same at this point, both end at US 1. US 1 is the former DH East Mainline and I would get serious about following it when I headed north but for now I set my sights on the Florida Keys.

**The end of the Tamiami Trail and Dixie Highway West at US 1 (Dec 26, 2008)**

The Dixie Highway never made it to the Keys. It ended, comfortably on the mainland, at Florida City. Further surface transportation was available during the Dixie's lifetime, however. Henry Flagler completed his Overseas Railroad to Key West in January of 1912. From then until September of 1935, steel rails tied Key West to the mainland. The connection was severed when the Labor Day Hurricane of 1935 took out about forty miles of the railroad. It was never rebuilt but a road for cars and trucks, the Overseas Highway, was built on the railroad's piers and opened in 1938.

I turned right in Miami and spent the night on Key Largo. I ended up making my Key West visit an extra long day trip and was back on the mainland for the next night. I returned to the Dixie Highway the following morning.

Although it appears that an extension or detour to Royal Palm State Park briefly existed on paper, Florida City is the generally accepted terminus and southernmost point of the Dixie Highway. That's where I spent the night and where I started my drive back to Cincinnati.

**Coral Castle, Homestead, FL (Dec 28, 2008)**

The Dixie Highway had a few years of official life left when Ed Leedskalnin started building Coral Castle in 1923 but it had probably been turned into US 1 by the time his masterpiece became a tourist attraction. Even so, visiting the coral building and sculptures is a pretty good kickoff for a drive from the DH terminus just a few miles south. There is no known explanation for how the 100 pound Leedskalnin moved and placed the huge stones and it is said that he always worked alone and at night. Maybe there were secret accomplices or maybe he possessed magic. Or maybe it was just that, as he claimed, he simply "understood the laws of weight and leverage". Whatever the method, it sure is impressive and it's all because the love of his life jilted him in 1913.

Road signed Old Dixie Highway can be driven near the castle and at quite a few other places in southern Florida though most of it bears little resemblance to the Dixie Highway of the 1920s. Even where the congestion of overbuilt coastal cities can be kept out of sight or at least out of frame, modern paving and signage rules out any chance of mistaking the scene for something from the DH's heyday.

**Old Dixie Highway in Delray Beach, FL (Dec 28, 2008)**

Asphalt pavement and an "old" in the name, along with a slightly futuristic water tower, clearly mark the Delray Beach picture as something recent but it does illustrate the natural tendency of early twentieth century roads to shadow the paths of railroads.

Where the path of the Dixie follows the coast, another difference between today and the 1920s occurred to me. I know that the Florida coastline was not devoid of manmade structures in the '20s but neither was it filled with a palisade of high-rise hotels and other buildings. From well south of Miami to well north of Fort Lauderdale, an ocean view is something more often associated with a tenth floor mini-suite than with the seat of a car. There are exceptions and it's not as if the ocean is totally blocked from view for the entire distance but I have to believe that traveling this road in the 1920s felt a lot more like driving alongside the Atlantic than it does today.

**Indian River Drive (Dixie Highway) south of Fort Pierce, FL (Dec 30, 2008)**

Moving on north, away from the big cities, increasingly opens things up. Pavement and such continue to keep any illusion of this being the 1920s at bay but you – or at least I – do start to feel the presence of the ocean in a way that someone in a Model T might have felt in 1920 something.

We may not always want to admit it and we probably don't even acknowledge it to ourselves all that often but illusion seeking is part of what makes us drivers-of-old-roads do what we do. It's rarely, if ever, the main reason, but it's there. Even people who only find themselves on an isolated stretch of old two-lane totally by accident sometimes can't help but try to imagine what is was like driving the road in the past. I'm pretty sure that most of us who drive old two-lanes on a regular basis do some imagining on a regular basis, too. I'm not particularly good at it. There are lots of folk who are much better. But I try and when it's a pioneer road like the Dixie Highway I try imagining what driving it was like when not only this specific road was new but the whole concept of roads and cars and driving was new.

Avoiding visible reminders of the present helps. Just north of Mims, one reminder, smooth asphalt, is absent. The illusion still isn't perfect. The road is probably wider and better graded than it ever was when the Dixie Highway Association held sway over it and signs in the distance look a little too modern. It is rather close, though.

**Unpaved Old Dixie Highway north of Mims, FL (Dec 29, 2008)**

Another sixty miles to the north is some Old Dixie Highway that feeds the illusion even better. It may not look exactly as it did when new but that's not because of any modernization. I believe that a description of the car I was driving will help with the story of my first contact with the road.

I was in a 2006 Corvette coupe. I had some second thoughts about it when I encountered freezing rain just after leaving Cincinnati but there were no problems and, once I got away from the cold weather, I was quite happy with my choice. It seemed just the car for the Tamiami Trail and the Overseas Highway to Key West. I knew that the weather could be nasty when I returned to Ohio but that was days away and nothing to worry about now. It never occurred to me that my closest brush with danger due to the no-clearance wide-tired rear-drive Chevy would be in sunny Florida.

A little more than a mile north of Brunnel, County Road 13 heads west from US 1 toward the town of Espanola. The three miles to Espanola are well maintained two-lane asphalt and asphalt continues through the town although it seems a little narrower and there are a few cracks here and there. There's not much in Espanola now but it once had its own post office, a hotel, and a restaurant. That was when the road through it was freshly paved with brick as part of the new Dixie Highway. The brick was laid in 1915 and the road bypassed by the new US 1 in 1926 or 1927. North of town it hasn't received much attention since then.

**Obviously brick Old Dixie Highway near Espanola, FL (Dec 30, 2008)**

I passed a "ROUGH ROAD" sign in the town but didn't give it much thought. Neither I nor the Corvette were strangers to rough roads and I figured I would just turn around, as I'd done before, if it got too rough. I was delighted when I spotted the first bricks. Brick roads are cool. At first the brick was showing in patches because it was partly covered by thin asphalt but before long it was sand that partly covered the brick. I noted this but didn't worry about it. As I drove on, the sand increased until an inch or two completely covered the bricks and it continued to get deeper. Without quite realizing it, I was driving on essentially pure sand. Now I was worried. Doubly so when a truck with tires only slightly smaller than Big Foot's passed me going the other way.

But worrying was about all I could do. The car was squirming a little but moving along and staying on the road. It seemed unlikely that I would get moving again if I stopped to turn around or calmly think things over so I kept moving. And worrying. I passed a turnoff but it looked like nothing more than a mud pit with a little sand mixed in. Turning onto it promised to be a frying pan to fire sort of thing. At last I spotted a space on the right where the grass had been flattened – probably by vehicles like the high-rise truck I'd seen earlier – but which had not yet been churned to mud. I used it to swing out far enough for a U-turn and, without a pause, headed back toward Espanola some three miles away.

**Not so obviously brick Old Dixie Highway near Espanola, FL (Dec 30, 2008)**

I returned to US 1 and circled around to the brick segment's north end where a fair amount of fully exposed brick paving could be seen. I looked it over and took pictures and even drove about a mile and a half of it but turned back as soon as the sand got more than a few grains deep. I know that nearly falling into the clutches of Florida sand won't be the last dumb thing I do but I like to at least space my really stupid moves out a little bit.

I'd driven about two miles of brick and sand from the south and almost that far from the north which left something around six miles for a future day. In truth, I'd actually driven about one mile of the southern section and squirmed along the other mile. I was feeling sort of proud of my escape as I sorted out the distances in the motel at the end of the day. Satellite imagery had been available for several years and that's where I turned to try to pinpoint my turnaround. Google Streetview was much newer. It had been introduced in May of 2007 and was still pretty much a novelty. I sure was surprised to see a blue line, indicating that Streetview imaging was available, running along the road out of Espanola. Sure enough, there on my computer screen, after a few clicks and a little scrolling, was an image, taken roughly one year before, of the very spot where I had made my deft and daring maneuver. Humbling? You bet. It's at N29° 32.8552' W81° 19.5660' for anyone wanting to take a look.

The rest of the day was uneventful as I followed the Dixie through Hastings and into Saint Augustine where I spent the night. I had visited Saint Augustine's most famous attraction, the three century old Castillo de San Marcos, before so chose to check out some other sights, like the 1874 lighthouse, this time. Of course, once I climbed the 219 steps to the top of the lighthouse, I could check out a whole lot of Saint Augustine.

Lighthouse, Saint Augustine, FL (Dec 30, 2008)

Heading north from Saint Augustine, the Dixie Highway angles away from the coast and toward Jacksonville. Jacksonville may not be as tall or congested as Miami but it is still a big city and one which I slipped through without stopping. The Dixie leaves town as US 17 and the US route more or less traces the path of the old highway all the way to Savannah. It overlaid a lot of the old road although some isolated scraps remain here and there where a curve has been straightened or the route shifted for some other reason.

**River Street, Savannah, GA (Jan 1, 2009)**

I reached Savannah in the late afternoon. It was New Year's Eve and I'm sure it was a happening place that night but I drove on through to quietly end 2008 in a motel at the north edge of town. I went back in to look it over on New Year's Day. The Dixie Highway doesn't reach the riverfront, where I did most of my looking over, but it does get within a couple of blocks. I saw enough of the Savannah riverfront to know that I like it and I ate shrimp & grits for the first time. I liked that, too.

**Unpaved Old Dixie Highway north of Springfield, GA (Jan 1, 2009)**

Georgia's Dixie Highway also has spots that fuel the illusion of being in an earlier time. One such spot is a short section of unpaved Old Dixie Highway about seven miles north of Springfield.

**Portland Concrete near Traveler's Rest, SC (Jan 2, 2009)**

More peeking into the past is possible a dozen miles north of Greenville, South Carolina, near Traveler's Rest where a short section of narrow concrete signed Old US Highway 25 can be driven. A half-dozen miles beyond that, a nearly fourteen mile long stretch of Old Highway departs from the current US 25. This section is paved with modern asphalt but still has the old ups and downs and curves. There is a Robert E. Lee and Dixie Highway marker, like the one I stumbled onto in November, where it crosses into North Carolina.

I continued on the Dixie into Asheville to the point where I had left it in November. I could now claim to have driven all of the DH East Mainline south of Cincinnati – with the notable exception of approximately six miles of sand covered brick near Espanola, Florida – as well as the southernmost 170 or so miles of the West Mainline. I had also made contact with another of the DH & Lee markers but missed several others in the area. I'll be back.

# 7 MORE BITS AND PIECES

After racking up quite a few Dixie Highway miles with that pair of trips at the end of 2008, my DH activity slacked off for a while. The summer of 2011 would be ending before I set off on another major outing on the road but I didn't ignore it. There were short additions in 2009 and '10 and another in the summer of 2011.

**Nickle Brothers service station, Powell, TN (Jul 2, 2009)**

The 2009 trip filled my Independence Day weekend. July 4th was on a Saturday which meant a day off Friday. I used Thursday evening to drive to Knoxville, Tennessee, and I naturally stopped by the Powell Airplane to see how it was doing. There were no huge changes but it was clear that the place was no longer abandoned. Small improvements had been made and new bricks stacked behind the building indicated that some bigger things were in the works.

On Friday, I headed to Chattanooga, Tennessee, where the steamboat *Delta Queen* had opened as a stationary hotel not quite a month before. I had missed out on cruising on the beautiful old sternwheeler and really looked forward to spending a couple of nights on board.

Despite the *Queen* having arrived in Chattanooga in February and not opening as a hotel until June, many of the boat's personnel remained in place and many of the dining and entertainment opportunities offered during cruises were still available dockside. My stay was as close to a cruising experience as I could have hoped for plus I got to see and hear an Independence Day concert and fireworks display from the *Queen*'s decks. But that was later, after I'd driven the Dixie Highway Tennessee Connector from Knoxville to Chattanooga.

Knoxville isn't a huge city but it is a city and the first several miles of the connector, which leaves Knoxville on US 70, are lined with city things such as stores and restaurants. It passes under both I-140 and I-75 and somewhere between the two it becomes fairly rural.

Just beyond I-75, what's left of Frank Kinger's gas station stands in a 'V' on the south side of the road where it's been since 1931. The triangular roof that connected the circular office with the big pillar out front hung on until at least 2004.

**Remains of Frank Kinger's service station near Pleasant View, TN (Jul 3, 2009)**

**Dixie Lee Highway underpass south of Rockwood, TN (Jul 3, 2009)**

Forty some miles west of Knoxville, US 27 comes in from the north and the two US highways run together for a couple of miles. When they split, the DH Tennessee Connector follows US 27 southward as US 70 continues westward. About five miles after the split, a narrow drivable section of the old road can be reached on the west side of US 27. This road is signed Dixie Lee Highway for some reason. It crosses under the Norfolk Southern Railroad through an underpass that I'm guessing is from the 1920s or '30s.

**William J. Bryan statue at Rhea County Courthouse, Dayton, TN (Jul 3, 2009)**

When I drove into Dayton, Tennessee, on a late Friday morning, the filled stalls of a farmer's market stood on a cross street by the courthouse. The sidewalk in front of the courthouse contains a timeline of county history put down in 2007 for the county's bicentennial. There are three entries on the timeline for 1925. The first, "Cumberland Coal & Iron Fails", notes the closing of a company that had been prosperous and significant in the late 1800s. The second is "Scopes Trial".

This is where John T. Scopes was tried and convicted of illegally teaching evolution in the local high school. Although no one else was ever charged under the newly enacted law, teaching evolution remained illegal in Tennessee for decades. The famous attorney Clarence Darrow served on the defense and the equally famous William Jennings Bryan was part of the prosecuting team. It's unlikely that Darrow will ever get a statue on the courthouse lawn but, eighty years after the trial, Bryan did. He didn't have much time to savor his victory back in 1925. The third timeline entry for the year is "W. J. Bryan Dies In Dayton". That was just five days after the trial ended.

I drove on to where the connector ended at the DH West Mainline in Chattanooga then headed off to have a wonderful Independence Day with no relationship to the Dixie Highway whatsoever.

**Horse Shoe Camp Motel near Bowling Green, KY (Sep 4, 2009)**

The road trip I was on just two months later had no real connection with the Dixie Highway, either, but it did take me to Bowling Green, Kentucky, and the long closed motel that I first saw in 2004. Five years later, the motel I used to mark the start of my affair with the Dixie looks only slightly more worn.

**Nickle Brothers service station, Powell, TN (Aug 28, 2010)**

In August, while on another non-DH road trip, I found myself spending the night at the north edge of Knoxville. That naturally led to a visit to the Powell Airplane where I saw no apparent changes.

**Restored Texaco Station, Cowan, TN (Sep 15, 2010)**

I drove some Dixie Highway in September of 2010 even though the trip I was on was not focused on the DH. I was in Chattanooga and wanted to be in Nashville and included the bit of DH West Mainline between Monteagle and Shelbyville when I made the move. The town of Cowan, with a nicely restored Texaco station and small railroad museum, made an interesting stop along the way.

**Horse Shoe Camp Motel near Bowling Green, KY (Sep 16, 2010)**

From Nashville, I headed home through Bowling Green, Kentucky, and, just as getting near Knoxville often results in a stop at the airplane shaped gas station north of town, getting near Bowling Green often results in a visit to the old motel north of that town. This time the stop wasn't pleasant. Barely a year had passed since my last visit but the year had not been kind to the old structure. The roof over the office had given way and the "MODERN COTTAGES" sign was tilting badly. It looked like the beginning of the end.

I began this story with memories of seeing Dixie Highway signs in Dayton, Ohio, then told of seeing more after moving to Cincinnati. I'd since driven between the two cities countless times and had no doubt seen the word "Dixie" so many times that it often didn't even register. I may have driven every inch of the Dixie Highway along the way though probably not. Even if I had, I had no way of knowing. I had never intentionally followed the Highway from one city to the other so, in July of 2011, I did just that.

**Intersection of National Road and Dixie Highway, Vandalia, OH (Jul 29, 2011)**

The occasion was the dedication of a memorial bench and informative sign near where the National Road and the Dixie Highway East Mainline (now signed Dixie Drive) once crossed in Vandalia, Ohio. A pair of small signs, mounted high above the roadway, label this "The Original Crossroads of America".

The title "Crossroads of America" certainly has no shortage of claimants. Adding the qualifier "original" narrows the field a bit while acknowledging that some newer intersection might be worthy of the title. Indiana laid claim to the title for the whole state by adopting it as its motto in 1937. By adding "original" to their sign, the folks in Vandalia could be giving a nod toward the Hoosier State's claim. Maybe, but not, I think, likely. When US Numbered Highways replaced the named auto trails, this bit of the National Road became US 40, this bit of the Dixie Highway became US 25, and the traffic continued to flow through the intersection. Relief came when I-70 and I-75, spiritual successors to US 40 and US 25, opened. Sorry, Hoosiers, but I'm pretty sure it was the crossing of the two interstates, less than two miles away, that Vandalians had in mind when they put the word "original" on their sign.

**Dixie Twin Drive-In, Dayton, OH (Jul 29, 2011)**

The name Dixie is not only retained in the street name but also shows up on some businesses along the way. An outstanding example is the Dixie Twin Drive-In with its classic sign, two screens, and, as of 2014, two state of the art digital projectors.

Between Dayton and Hamilton the Dixie Highway stays fairly close to the Great Miami River. As it passes through river towns such as Moraine, Franklin, and Middletown, traffic is split onto a pair of one way streets. This is a fairly common approach to dealing with increased traffic levels. In Franklin this results in southbound traffic being routed onto River Street away from Main Street and the original path of the Dixie Highway. I mention this because of the murals. In conjunction with Ohio's bicentennial in 2003, Franklin had the well known artist Eric Henn paint a number of murals in the town. The murals depict various periods of Franklin's history and are sometimes made extra realistic with the addition of real world items like lights or a clock. Even though my purpose on this day was to drive the Dixie Highway south, I just had to drive this section both ways so I could see the murals.

**Mural on Dixie Highway in Franklin, OH (Jul 29, 2011)**

From Hamilton to Cincinnati, the current Ohio Route 4 essentially follows the path of the DH and that's what I drove. I made my way to the Roebling Bridge using Vine Street and some guesswork. As they should have been, the named auto trails were more concerned with getting motorists between towns rather than through them. Determining the official path, or if there even was one, through any given city isn't easy. I've since decided that the path I followed through Cincinnati on this day was probably not right. So, although I gave myself credit for the full drive at the end of the day, I would later revoke part of it and come back to do it right.

Following my not-quite-right drive to the Ohio River, I made my way back to the north side of the city to drive another possible alignment northbound. I say possible because, although multiple sources talk of an alignment that passed through West Chester and Monroe rather than Middletown and Hamilton and there are some Dixie Highway street signs along the way, there seems to be no mention of this second alignment in official DHA documents. Maybe it was just one of those things that slipped through the cracks as the association reached the end of its life or maybe locals took it upon themselves to name things however they saw fit. Regardless of the route's legitimacy, I decided to play it safe and, after picking up this alternate alignment at the Butler-Hamilton county line, I followed it to the point of the split south of Franklin.

# 8 THE NORTHERNEST

The year 2011 was going to be the one in which I finally saw Boston. I even had some tour and motel reservations in place with plans to start driving east on August 27. On August 20, Tropical Storm Irene was identified near the Lesser Antilles. After striking several islands, she reached North Carolina as a Category 1 Hurricane on my scheduled departure date. By then I'd made some changes. I started driving on the 27th but headed north rather than east.

I had previously plotted most of the Dixie Highway so, when the east coast trip became undoable, I substituted a longish DH one. Starting at Vandalia's Original Crossroads of America that I'd driven south from just a month before, I now drove north. Much like on that south bound trip, the road I drove at the start of this one was hardly new to me. I'd driven most or all of the Ohio portion at least once but, also like that southbound trip, never with the intent of following the Dixie Highway.

In 1936, the Dayton Municipal Airport opened in the northwest corner of the Original Crossroads of America. The main entrance to the airport is on US 40, National Road, but there is an entrance on Dixie Drive that provides access to the Dayton Air Show, one of the nation's best, each year.

There's more aeronautical history a few miles further on at WACO Field near Troy. Waco Aircraft Company (originally founded in 1920 as Weaver Aircraft Company) was hitting its stride as the Dixie was fading. It was the world's largest manufacturer of passenger planes for several years around 1930. The annual fly-in fills the field with some of the most beautiful biplanes ever made.

**WACO Field, Troy, OH (Aug 27, 2011)**

About twenty miles north of Troy, the town of Sidney is home to a couple of landmarks with DH era connections. First up is the Big Four Bridge at the south edge of town. The massive concrete bridge opened in 1924 to carry the Cleveland, Cincinnati, Chicago, and St. Louis Railway (a.k.a. The Big Four Railway) over the Great Miami River and Sidney's Main Avenue which was the Dixie Highway at the time. Next to the big column east of the highway, an informative sign, bearing a Shelby County Historical Society imprint, gives credence to an oft heard rumor with the statement "An unidentified worker is believed to be buried in the column behind this marker."

**Big Four Bridge, Sidney, OH (Aug 27, 2011)**

**The Spot to Eat, Sidney, OH (Aug 27, 2011)**

In downtown Sidney, "The Spot" was waiting when the Dixie Highway arrived. It was started in 1907 by a man named Spot Miller who took the wheels off of his parked chuck-wagon to comply with city ordinances. It has gone through several iterations and quite a few owners but continues to serve good food across the corner from the courthouse. The DH ran one block east of here but I'm sure many who traveled it ate at the chuck-wagon which was in place until 1934. Today, thanks to one-way streets, southbound DH travelers drive right by "The Spot".

Wapakoneta is about twenty miles north of Sidney. The smooth two-lane that connects the two passes through the towns of Anna and Botkins and lots of Ohio farmland. These days, Wapakoneta is no doubt best known as the home of the first man on the moon, Neil Armstrong. There is a moon-shaped Armstrong Air & Space museum at the east edge of town near the expressway. The normal complement of fast-food restaurants, gas stations, and chain stores are out there, too. Downtown, however, probably looks a lot like it did during Neil's childhood.

**Wapa Theater, Wapakoneta, OH (Aug 27, 2011)**

The wonderful neon trimmed Wapa Theater marquee went up in 1938. The building it hangs from went up in 1904. It was originally called the Brown Theater, a name that still appears at the top of the structure, and presented vaudeville shows. That's what would have been available to travelers on the Dixie Highway that passed right by the doors. There are several other old and interesting buildings along the DH in downtown Wapakoneta including one, the Alpha Café, with a huge back bar carved in 1893.

The city of Lima is about a dozen miles north. Prior to 1919, the Lincoln Highway crossed the Dixie Highway in downtown Lima creating another candidate for Crossroads of America. Of course, yet another candidate was created in 1919 when the Lincoln moved five miles north to cross the Dixie in Beaver Dam. The Beaver Dam crossing has a little something extra going for it. The south leg of the DH reached Beaver Dam on the west side of town while the north leg connected at the east edge. This resulted in the Lincoln and Dixie Highways running on top of each other for about a third of a mile.

There are a few more jogs like the one in Beaver Dam but the northbound Dixie Highway generally travels northeast between Lima and Findlay. From Findlay, it strikes out almost directly north to Perrysburg. The outing took on a slightly different flavor when I got out of my home state a few miles north of Toledo.

**Dixie Soft Serve Ice Cream, Monroe, MI (Aug 28, 2011)**

I long ago came to grips with seeing the word "Dixie" on signs in Ohio. I'm barely over the line so it shouldn't be a big deal but we Buckeyes think of Michigan as the cold north, lower Canada. Seeing an ice cream stand in Michigan brought a smile to my face. Seeing "Dixie" in the name turned it into a grin.

**Facing north on Woodward Avenue,  Detroit, MI (Aug 28, 2011)**

The Dixie Highway East Mainline turns left in downtown Detroit and heads northwest toward Flint. There is a loop that cuts off not far from Cadillac Square and runs northeast along Lake Huron to Harbor Beach but that will have to wait for another trip. Today I'm following the East Mainline along Woodward Avenue.

In 2009, the U.S. Department of Transportation designated Woodward Avenue an All-American Road. The sources of Woodward's fame are many and varied. During the era of named auto trails, it carried the Theodore Roosevelt International Highway as well as the Dixie Highway. It's where Detroit holds its Thanksgiving Day Parade, tied for second oldest in the nation, and home to the wild and wonderful Woodward Dream Cruise which has been called "the largest single-day classic car event in the world". It is also where the nation's "first mile of concrete highway" was built. It was not the first time concrete was used as paving in the U.S. That was in Bellefontaine, Ohio, in 1891 and it also appeared on some streets in other cities before being laid down on Woodward in 1909. The words "mile" and "highway" in the claim are important. The section was roughly six miles from the center of town and clearly qualified as a road or highway rather than a street. Being a full mile long also distinguished it from the shorter lengths inside cities. It was the seedling mile of seedling miles. It went over so well that the entire road from Detroit to Pontiac, a distance of 27 miles, was paved with concrete in 1916. A few years later, in 1923, this was made into a "super highway" with a 40 foot median separating four lanes in each direction.

Today it is hardly pastoral. There really isn't much that feels at all rural until somewhere north of Flint. By then Woodward Avenue has changed to Saginaw Road with the Dixie Highway name appearing now and then. But, even though farmland often lines the road instead of tall buildings and the wide median is gone, the pavement continues to be at least two lanes each way.

**Dixie Motor Speedway near Birch Run, MI (Aug 28, 2011)**

Michigan is where the U.S. auto industry reached its peak and it is certainly one of the racingest states in the union. I'm following the Dixie Highway with the occasional sign identifying it as such. At some intellectual level I know the sign is completely logical, yet, seeing a Michigan race track with "Dixie" in its name and stock cars on its sign, made me grin just like that ice cream stand in Monroe.

**Detour near Bridgeport, MI (Aug 28, 2011)**

My grinning was cut short by a bank of signs less than five miles up the road. I eased around the barricade to check out the local businesses – and get as close to the river as possible – then did the same thing on the other side. A new bridge is now in place so I could go back and fill this in but, for now, there's a river wide gap in my Dixie Highway coverage here.

The Dixie Highway loses its identity as it enters Saginaw and it won't get it back for quite some time. It becomes Genesee Avenue at Saginaw's south edge then goes through a variety of names as it passes through Bay City and moves north along the shore of Lake Huron. Near Standish the Dixie and US 23 hook up and together hug the shore even tighter. East of Omer, which calls itself "Michigan's Smallest City", the road narrows to two lanes for what seems like the first time since way south of Detroit. The lake is often visible but rarely accessible. Apparently most, if not all, of the shoreline is privately owned. One exception lies north of Harrisville at Sturgeon Point State Park. The park and the 1870 lighthouse are a little over a mile from the Dixie Highway but the drive is easily justified by cool views of both tower and lake.

**Sturgeon Point Lighthouse (Aug 29, 2011)**

**Nick's Southside Diner, Alpena, MI (Aug 29, 2011)**

The town of Alpena is one of the few places where the lake front is reachable. In fact, it is possible to get fed and get lakeside without leaving the Dixie Highway. After personally refueling at Al's Diner (actually Nick's Southside Diner) as I entered Alpena, I was happy to stop at one of the lakefront parks where relaxing and staring at the water just come naturally. That diner, by the way, is a 1955 O'Mahony.

**Dixie Highway south of Rogers City, MI (Aug 29, 2011)**

Above Alpena, the road turns to the west with the curve of the shore. Along the way, it hints at the tree lined two-lane I had subconsciously expected. I believe that, prior to this trip, Flint had been the most northern point in Michigan I'd ever visited by car. I had two images in mind for roads outside the cities. To me, Michigan was cars, lakes, and trees. I had been to Detroit several times and visited The Henry Ford a few times before it was called that. I had even attended the Woodward Dream Cruise once upon a time. I felt I'd had a reasonable amount of exposure to the car side of Michigan. Now I was ready for lakes and trees.

I saw a little of the state's lake side once I'd passed Au Gres. There were no long stretches of open shoreline and what separated the short stretches from each other was often homes or commercial buildings but there were places along the way where water stretched to the horizon. It wasn't precisely what I'd conjured up in my head but it was close enough. There had been, however, no unbroken line of trees stretching to the horizon. Like the recent views of the lake had not precisely matched the image I'd cooked up, the tree lined road I now saw as I headed west wasn't precisely what I'd imagined, either. But, it too was close enough. Tall stately pines close by the roadside would have been better but there were trees and it was two-lane and it wasn't downtown Detroit or Flint.

**One time Dixie Highway terminus in Mackinaw City, MI (Aug 29, 2011)**

Despite its name, Mackinaw City isn't a city. It's a village. With a population of just over 800, it seems the right size to be a village but there is obviously more to it than that. Michigan has several cities whose population is less than Mackinaw City's (The aforementioned Omer had just 313 residents in 2010.) and villages which are many times larger. Mackinaw City's population explodes in the summer. It is a major tourist destination with forty or so motels plus a fair number of B&Bs and vacation rentals. There are definitely places where it feels like a city but the larger motels are at the edges so the older part of town still feels pretty much like a village. Of course, it's a village where the shops mostly sell fudge, T-shirts, and souvenirs.

**Dixie Highway Apex Marker, Mackinaw City, MI (1916)**

The Dixie Highway once ended in front of the Dixie Saloon – sort of. Actually, according to a marker that once stood about where the clock does now, this was the "apex" of the Dixie Highway. Erected in 1916, it also marked the coming together of the East Michigan Pike (which was sorta kinda the DH East Mainline) and the West Michigan Pike (which was sorta kinda the DH Northern Connector). When the DHA quietly demoted Chicago and started talking about a single northern terminus, this is where the Eastern and Western Divisions split. The marker was built of stones donated by and representing "every man, woman, and child within a radius of 10 miles". It was removed in the 1950s and all those stones were tossed into the lake. The northern terminus or "apex" was officially moved to Sault Sainte Marie in September 1921 although there are indications it was unofficially moved much earlier.

Before 1957, anyone heading to Sault Sainte Marie from Mackinaw City needed some sort of boat whether their destination was an official terminus or not. From the time the Dixie Highway was extended to and through Michigan's upper peninsula, until the Dixie Highway Association disbanded, ferries made up the section across the Straits of Mackinac. DH travelers hitched rides on railroad ferries until a separate automobile service began in 1923.

**Mackinac Bridge from south end (Aug 30, 2011)**

Automobile ferries ceased operation in 1957 when the 1.6 mile long (5 miles including approaches) Mackinac Bridge opened. The last rail ferry shut down in 1984, not because a bridge replaced it but because rail service to Saint Ignace simply ended.

When I drove this section in 2011, the only directions I had were for southbound travel and consisted of "Start in Sault Ste. Marie, MI, and follow MI 129 south". From that, I anticipated reaching the terminus by following MI 129 north to its end. In practice, however, there was a problem. MI 129 currently ends when it reaches I-75B on Ashmun Street. That is over a mile and a half from the waterfront and just couldn't be right. MI-129 and the Dixie Highway had surely reached the heart of the city in pre-interstate days. So I decided they probably both ended with Ashmun Street and further decided that Ashmun ended about where the tank-treaded backhoe is in the photograph of the blocked off street. Pavement continues across the street but it is a parking lot entrance. I have since seen a guide book with southbound directions commencing at Ashmun and Portage which is essentially where I stood to take the picture. Northbound directions end one block to the west. Had I taken a selfie that day, I might have captured a glimpse of the Dixie Highway terminus. As it is, not exactly.

**Probably not Dixie Highway terminus (Aug 30, 2011)**

I really enjoyed my brief stay in Sault Sainte Marie. I took a boat tour which headed west through a lock on the American side then east through one on the Canadian side. I found a motel across the street from the American lock and was able to watch several boats go through including some at night. I dined on fresh whitefish washed down with beer from a newly opened brewery. In the morning, before returning south, I crossed the border for exotic adventure in a foreign land.

So maybe Canada isn't all that exotic and maybe Sault Sainte Marie, Ontario, isn't overflowing with adventure but I enjoyed it. I had a meal and a Molson then stopped by the lock I had passed through the day before. By pure luck, as I stood by the lock, I saw the *Hiawatha*, the tour boat I had ridden in, approaching and was able to watch it lock through. Observers can get right up to the side of the lock and walkways even allow crossing over the gates when they are closed. Security is nothing like it is on the American side. This is partially due to the fact that no cargo passes through the Canadian lock and partially due (I'll admit I'm guessing here.) to Canadians simply not being as uptight as we are.

I reentered the United States without incident and retraced my path to Mackinaw City where I turned west on the Dixie Highway Northern Connector. The route of the connector was largely adopted by US 31. For twenty-some miles, it heads almost directly south then turns to the west near Alanson. After reaching Lake Michigan near Bay View, it pretty much hugs the shore to Traverse City.

**Old US 31 west of Bay View, MI (Sep 1, 2011)**

About a half dozen miles west of Bay View, a couple miles of Old US 31 can be driven along the south side of the current route. This would have once been Dixie Highway and is a great chance to experience that "driving in the '20s" illusion.

First World's Largest Cherry Pie, Charlevoix, MI (Sep 1, 2011)

Second World's Largest Cherry Pie, Traverse City, MI (Sep 2, 2011)

This is cherry country. I suppose I was aware of that at some level but seeing the pan used to bake the World's Largest Cherry Pie brought it front and center. A small park in the town of

Charlevoix displays the pan used to bake a 17,420 pound pie in 1976. This was the First World's Largest Cherry Pie. Less than fifty miles away, in Traverse City, the pan used to bake the Second World's Largest Cherry Pie is on display. The Second World's Largest (i.e., the one that took the title from the first) weighed in at 28,350 pounds. The Charlevoix pie reigned from 1976 to 1987. The Traverse City pie's reign was shorter. It was dethroned in 1992 by a 39,683 pounder baked in Oliver, British Columbia, Canada. The Third World's Largest Cherry Pie pan is not on display.

The road turns away from the lake as it leaves Traverse City. Some twenty-five miles later it passes through the village of Honor. It might sound like a place built on bravery or scholarship or some other highly desirable trait, but the name actually came from the daughter of a corporate bigwig back when this was a huge logging area. Today it is a big trout and salmon area. Honor calls itself Coho Capital and hosts the National Coho Festival each year. It wasn't the name that first caught my eye but a number of nicely maintained older motels at least two of which featured separate "motor court" style cabins. I'm guessing fishers provide the business that keeps those motels looking so good.

**Cherry Bowl Drive In, Honor, MI (Sep 2, 2011)**

Even though it was the motels and cabins that first caught my attention, it was the Cherry Bowl that hung onto it. Any establishment with a Corvair and a giant chicken out front is OK by me, drive-in theaters doubly so. And I've learned good things about the Cherry Bowl since my 2011 drive-by.

In 2013, as the movie industry moved ever closer to digital only distribution, Honda set out to help some theaters with the expensive transition. The goal of their Project Drive-In was to give new $80,000 projectors to five drive-in theaters selected by the public. Donations made during the voting ultimately allowed a total of nine projectors to be awarded. Dayton, Ohio's, Dixie Drive-In, which I mentioned in chapter seven, didn't make the cut but managed to upgrade on their own. The Cherry Bowl was one of the lucky nine. That's much more than an honor. It's a lifeline.

**Division Street/CR A-45 south of Grand Rapids, MI (Sep 3, 2011)**

I encountered rain soon after leaving Honor and divided four-lane soon after passing Ludington. The road moves closer to Lake Michigan and generally follows the shoreline south but it never really gets into hugging it before turning inland towards Grand Rapids. I spent the night in Grand Rapids while the rain moved on. In the morning, I found some pleasant and dry two-lane a few miles south of town. The quality of the paving and the scenery varies but the road remains two-lane and mildly scenic to Kalamazoo. After the normal blast of multi-lane city streets, the two-lane returns west of town. MI 51 picks up the path of the Dixie Highway about twenty miles west of Kalamazoo and carries it to the Indiana line. It, too, is almost all enjoyable two-lane.

South Bend, Indiana, is barely across the state line and I was barely into South Bend before that enjoyable two-lane became just a memory. It took several blocks of crawling along with the intense traffic for me to realize that it wasn't a ten car pileup causing the congestion. It was something much bigger than that. I had entered South Bend just hours before a Notre Dame football game.

I eventually worked my way through the pre-game crush in South Bend and headed south on US 31, a.k.a. Michigan Road, a.k.a. Dixie Highway. There is a parting of the ways at Rochester with US 31 angling southwest toward Kokomo and the Dixie, the Michigan, and me angling southwest toward Logansport on IN 25.

**Dinner at Char-Bett Drive-In, Logansport, IN (Sep 3, 2011)**

By the time I reached Logansport, I was ready for dinner and the Char-Bett Drive-In at the city's north edge seemed like just the place. Named after founders Charlie and Betty Streu, the place has been serving up 'burgers, fries, and all the rest since 1958. Car hops and a walk-up window. Just like the good old days.

The Michigan Road has been around a long time. It was the first road commissioned by the Indiana state government and that was back in 1826. Running between the Indiana towns of Madison on the Ohio River and Michigan City on Lake Michigan, it connected the north and south edges of the state with each other and with the new capital in the center. When the Dixie Highway came along, it was no doubt a very sensible thing for the newcomer to follow the established route where possible. It does just that all the way to Indianapolis.

I drove part of this section back in 2008 and spoke of it in chapter 4. Things were much better planned this time but I still missed out on a meal at White House #1 in downtown Logansport. I had targeted the place for breakfast and actually thought I had done the required research and scheduling. However, between 2008 and this visit, they had changed from closing on Monday and Tuesday to closing on Sunday and Monday. Yeah, it was Sunday.

Sycamore Row south of Logansport, IN (Sep 4, 2011)

The three of us, the Michigan Road, the Dixie Highway Northern Connector, and I, left Logansport on IN 29. About ten miles south of town, two lines of trees stand to the west of the current road with a strip of asphalt running between them. A sign identifies this as Sycamore Row. Until 1987, that strip of asphalt carried IN 29. The sign also describes the rows of sycamores as having "…sprouted from freshly cut logs used to corduroy…" a section of road. Other stories about the origin of the trees exist. They can't all be true, of course, but regardless of how the trees got there, it is undeniable that they have been there a long time (witnesses have reported that the trees were there at least as far back as 1868) and that an awful lot of transportation history has passed between them.

Quite a surprise awaited me at the end of the Dixie Highway Northern Connector. To be truthful it was just a bit beyond the end of the connector as I drove a section of DH West Mainline to reach the DH Midwestern Connector. The centerpiece of Indianapolis, of the whole state in fact, is the Soldiers and Sailors Monument in the center of Monument Circle. It was directly in front of me and it did not look right. There seemed to be some sort of scaffolding at the top of the column and a crane stood beside it. Bumper to bumper traffic filled the Circle. As I passed through the Circle and snapped some photos, the connection between the scaffolding and the crane and a large street side figure became apparent. It would be much later, however, that I learned the full story.

Construction started in 1888, the column was completed in 1892, and the bronze sculpture that would eventually be called Victory hoisted to the top in 1893. There she stood while the rest of the monument was completed and finally dedicated on May 15, 1902. Daring workmen occasionally scaled the statue to make inspections and small repairs but Victory never left her post at the top of the 284.5 foot monument. Then, in early 2011, it was determined that she really needed to go "back to the shop" and on April 23 she was lifted off of her pedestal inside protective framework. Now she was back and patiently posing for photos until time to return to the spot from where she had seen, among other things, the Dixie Highway come and go without batting an eye.

**Restored Victory statue, Indianapolis, IN (Sep 4, 2011)**

**DH Connector approaching downtown Dayton, OH (Sep 4, 2011)**

The trip ended in Dayton about nine miles south of where it started. The Dixie Highway Midwestern Connector and the National Old Trails Road share a route between Indianapolis and Dayton. I've driven it before but not as the Dixie Highway. The National Road, where the trip started, was plotted along an arrow straight line between Columbus, the capital of Ohio, and Indianapolis, the capital of Indiana. Federal funding for road construction ended forty some miles west of Columbus at Springfield. Private turnpike companies stepped in to provide a way to the west but they did it by going where the people were rather than where the National Road guidelines dictated. The "Dayton Cutoff" connected Springfield, Dayton, and Eaton, Ohio, with Richmond, Indiana. When the National Old Trails Road Association was picking its path across the country, it went where the better roads were and that was through Dayton, nine miles south of Vandalia and the National Road.

# 9 TALLY TIME

My encounters with the Dixie Highway were now more planned than accidental with some attention given to following a historically accurate route. My DH travels were recorded in a little text file so I could tell what I had driven. It had lines like

```
Y   Bowling Green - Russellville
N - Russellville - Nashville
```

to show that I had driven the route between Bowling Green and Russellville but not between Russellville and Nashville. It worked but it didn't provide much of a feel for what I'd covered and even less for what remained.

According to the Dixie Highway Association, the total mileage for the system was 5,786. The routes I had plotted to approximate the system on modern roads was 6,056. I did not investigate the 270 mile discrepancy but merely attributed it to the near century time difference. Based on those plotted routes, when I completed the drive to the apex, I had driven 3,254 miles of Dixie Highway. I was over half way there but which half? My list of Ys and Ns and city pairs held the answer but it wasn't easy to see and it was far from easy to imagine how a planned road trip might relate. I needed something visual.

**Driven Dixie Highway score in September 2011**

Thinking myself quite clever, I took a copy of the Dixie Highway Association outline map shown in chapter 2 and colored the sections I had driven in green. That worked for one more trip.

That next trip was probably even influenced a bit by the marked up map. Nashville, Tennessee, was a strong candidate for a Christmas destination and it almost certainly got elevated a little when I saw it was in the center of a non-green stretch of Dixie Highway. That was a surprise. I was no stranger to Nashville but apparently had never knowingly entered or exited on the DH. There were many other reasons for organizing the trip around Nashville but that fact didn't hurt.

The undriven stretch started at Russellville, Kentucky, and ended at Shelbyville, Tennessee. Rain that was sometimes heavy really interfered with sightseeing to and through Nashville. I sometimes hear people talk about being slowed down by rain but I think my own, already slow, pace is often increased by it. When rain is falling there is much less temptation to stop and take pictures.

**Wat Lao Buddhist Temple north of Murfreesboro, TN (Dec 22, 2011)**

The rain did let up south of Nashville but there was still some spotty drizzle and the world looked pretty dull. When I posted a photo of the Buddhist temple near Murfreesboro in my online journal I joked that it was the only thing with enough color to show through the gray.

My next contact with the Dixie Highway was really short. It was a redo triggered by Robert E. Lee. Back in November of 2008, on the way to Asheville, North Carolina, I found a marker dedicated to Robert E. Lee and the Dixie Highway and eventually learned that a total of ten were known to exist. Most are in the south but one is in Ohio less than twenty miles from my home. I may have driven by it multiple times and believed that I must have done so in July. How could I not see it? On a cold but clear January day, I set out to find the marker and correct a couple of other things, too.

In July, I had tried to follow the original Dixie Highway from Vandalia to Cincinnati and also tried to trace a later alignment northbound. That combination and a wrong turn helped explain missing the marker.

**Robert E. Lee and Dixie Highway marker near Franklin, OH (Jan 15, 2012)**

While southbound in July, I had turned right just a little too soon. I had passed the marker on the northbound part of that July drive but had missed it because it is partially hidden by bushes and I would have had to look behind me to see it. Driving a third of a mile further south before turning put me and the marker face to face.

When I wrote about that July outing, I admitted that I had almost certainly botched getting through Cincinnati. I had a little more information and mulled things over a bit more and thought I might be able to correct that, too. The best description I now had of the later alignment, the one I had partially driven northbound in July, had it connecting with the older alignment near the north edge of Cincinnati and both alignments following Reading Road all the way down town. That makes sense and answers questions I had about the two alignments fitting together. It is what I drove today.

**Lincoln sculpture at Rockdale & Reading, Cincinnati, OH (Jan 15, 2012)**

If anyone had asked me if I had ever visited the Lincoln statue at Rockdale and Reading, I'd have said yes. I would have been wrong. I had driven by it countless times and it seemed so familiar that I convinced myself that I had stood in front of it but, as I parked the car and walked to the statue on this day, I realized I was doing it for the first time.

The statue is in Avondale where 92% of the residents are black. Riots rocked the area in both 1967 and 1968. The 1967 riots sprang from a rally held at the base of this very statue. I knew these things although I had to be reminded. I even knew that the kneeling figure holds a quill pen and has just written "With malice toward none". I'm guessing that was mentioned in a news story or two. I did not know the source of the statue.

The statue was the work of William Granville Hastings and the gift of Captain Charles Clinton. Clinton's title came from his service in the Civil War. He also served as superintendent of the U.S. Mint in New Orleans and as Louisiana's auditor before moving to Cincinnati in 1887. Clinton had known and admired Lincoln and gave the statue to the Avondale school "…to incite the minds of boys that are and are to be to look into the character, and work and life and death of Mr. Lincoln."

That was in 1902. Two years later Clinton gave an identical statue to the town of Bunker Hill, Illinois, which had been the home of many of the soldiers who served under him in the war. The bases for both statues were paid for through local donations. Two copies of the statue, minus the kneeling figure, exist in Iowa. There is no apparent connection between these and Captain Clinton. One is on the Lincoln Highway in Jefferson and the other in Sioux City.

The artist, Hastings, died of "cancer of the stomach" in 1902 before the first statue was dedicated. He was 34. Clinton ended a letter explaining his gift with, "I am 72 years old to-day. Whatever I am to do I must be about it."

**Interior of Nickle Brothers service station, Powell, TN (Jan 27, 2012)**

Before January ended, I was headed back toward Florida. The destination was Lake Alfred where an uncle was wintering and a free bed awaited. The front end was I-75 but I took time to stop by the Powell Airplane and really lucked out by finding one of the volunteer workers on site. That wasn't the only surprise. A recover of the exterior with new galvanized steel was almost complete, I got to see inside where lots of rotting wood had been replaced, and I was able to buy a T-shirt. The old plane is sure looking good.

**Old Tampa Road near Loughman, FL (Jan 28, 2012)**

I abandoned the expressway in Orlando in order to follow the DH West Mainline through Kissimmee to Haines City. Penfield Street in Kissimmee has some well maintained brick pavement but I actually liked the not so well maintained brick of Old Tampa Road near Loughman better. It has been patched and possibly widened with asphalt and is a fairly rough ride but the close trees and some rather isolated segments allow a little of that old road feel to take hold. However, the cherry, or maybe the orange slice, on top of the sundae is the marker at the Polk County line.

In 1930, Polk County erected three markers welcoming travelers to the county and letting them know that this was citrus country. At least that was the intent. On one side of the Loughman area marker, citrus is misspelled. The eighty-five year old "typo" adds a certain charm to the already quaint scene and makes it one of my favorite roadside attractions.

**Polk County marker near Loughman, FL (Jan 28, 2012)**

It was great to be away from the Ohio winter and my uncle and I spent a lot of time doing nothing beyond retelling family stories. We did poke around a bit of the Dixie Highway Tampa-Saint Petersburg Loop that passed nearby and one day I drove down to Bok Gardens. Euchre games filled a couple of evenings and a cruise around the lake on a neighbor's boat filled an afternoon. I did have one mission on my mind, though, and one day we headed toward the coast to fulfill it.

Our first destination was the area around Mims where we checked out some potential locations for a possible Robert E. Lee and Dixie Highway marker. The clues had been weak and our expectations low so we weren't very disappointed when we found nothing. We played back road tourists and worked our way up the coast. Sometimes on old Dixie Highway. Sometimes not. North of Daytona we drove through the tunnel-like trees at Tomoka State Park then onto US 1. Just north of Bunnell we turned toward Espanola just as I had a little more than three years before. My mission was to drive those six miles of sand covered brick I had been happy to escape from in 2008. I was now in an AWD Subaru and the mission was accomplished in short order and with no drama. It was, nonetheless, satisfying.

If we had not done the Espanola drive during my stay, I would have done it on the way home. With it out of the way, my thoughts returned to that Tampa-Saint Petersburg Loop that connected with the West Mainline near Haines City and when I waved goodbye to my uncle that's the course I set off on.

The loop follows a fairly direct course from Haines City to Tampa. Between Haines City and Lake Alfred, it carries the name Old Dixie Highway and that name, along with just plain Dixie Highway, reappears around Auburndale. Then it's Old Tampa Highway to the county line where it climbs onto US 92. A Polk County Welcome marker, with all words spelled correctly, stands beside US 92. West of Plant City, the DH breaks from the US route and heads onto Ybor City on state and county roads.

**Nicahabana Cigars, Ybor City, FL (Feb 3, 2012)**

I took a break in Ybor City and even found a local brewpub. The bartender recommended Nicahabana Cigars as the place to buy hand rolled cigars so I picked up a few for friends. A fellow I met in front of the store recommended their Café Cubano so I gave it a try. Zoom. Zoom.

Barely a mile away, the Dixie Highway went right through the center of downtown Tampa. It passed over the north edge of the bay, dropped south to Saint Petersburg, then back north along the coast. I tolerated the city traffic but was not unhappy to see things thinning out as I reached the northern edge. When I decided that Tampa was on my route home, I had dropped a note to a friend living just north of town and things were coming together for a dinner meeting. With Tampa and Saint Petersburg both behind me, I was ready and the meeting clicked.

**Old Dixie Highway north of Hudson, FL (Feb 4, 2012)**

As I moved on north on US 19A in the morning, I was pleased to see Dixie Highway signs from time to time. A short stretch bears the name just south of the Pinellas-Pasco County line and it is also on several miles at Hudson. There is no bumpy patched pavement here. These roads are used frequently and well maintained.

**Weeki Wachee Mermaids (Feb 4, 2012)**

Not far from the signed Old Dixie Highway at Hudson, the loop, now back on US 19, passes one of the truly outstanding roadside attractions of all time. I was barely six months old when mermaids began performing at Weeki Wachee Springs so I've literally been waiting almost my entire life to see them. This is exactly what a road named Dixie Highway should lead to.

The northbound DH Tampa-Saint Petersburg Loop has roughly seventy-five miles to go when it leaves Weeki Wachee. It heads east on FL 50 then north on US 41 to Dunnellon where it moves onto state and county roads to reach Ocala and the DH West Mainline. I touched the Mainline but did not climb aboard. I said so long to the Dixie and headed home on I-75. I would have a problem to solve when I got there.

I'd known of the problem for some time but chose to ignore it as long as I could. The problem was the one I hinted at early in this chapter when I said my scoring method would work for one more trip. The trip it worked for was the rainy trip through Nashville. When it was done, I colored some more of my map green and all was well.

Technically there was a problem with the following trip but I made it go away. Only one of the two alignments between Franklin and Cincinnati appeared on the DHA map I was marking my travels on but, since they had not existed simultaneously, I decided that was not an issue. I need only mark one and the earlier alignment was just fine for that purpose.

But this latest problem could not be dealt with so easily. The entire Tampa-Saint Petersburg Loop was absent from the map. Here was more than 200 miles of Dixie Highway that I had driven and wanted to record but didn't know how. The case of the missing loop would resurface later but for the present I was concerned only with scoring my drives and I solved that by making my own map.

Although I prefer the word "streamlined" calling the map "crude" is not exactly wrong. The roads of my map were straight lines between key points and there were indeed curves and turns missing and even a few small towns but, more importantly, the DH Tampa-Saint Petersburg Loop was included. That loop, by the way, accounted for about 240 of the 270 mile difference between the DHA total and mine. I would now use this map to record and report my progress in driving the Dixie Highway.

**Driven Dixie Highway score in February 2012**

# 10 YET MORE BITS AND PIECES

The year was almost over before I added more Dixie Highway to my tally. It was a trip that celebrated Christmas in Chattanooga and the New Year in Raleigh with an Atlanta stop in between. I drove that fun bit of Dixie Highway between the Tennessee state line and Caryville on the way to Chattanooga for maybe the fourth or fifth time but rolled past Knoxville without checking in on the Powell Airplane.

In Chattanooga I spent three nights aboard the *Delta Queen* and did a little sightseeing. I visited the Lookout Mountain Battlefield for the first time and rode the Chattanooga Incline for the second. Christmas dinner was an outstanding buffet aboard the *Queen*.

The Dixie Highway West Mainline passes through Chattanooga and the Rome Loop begins there. I could drive the mainline as far as Atlanta but that would still leave a lot of it undriven so I decided to follow the Rome Loop on this trip and save the West Mainline segment for a future outing. The Rome Loop follows US 27 all the way to Rome, Georgia, and passes though the center of the Chickamauga and Chattanooga National Military Park. The Lookout Mountain Battlefield that I visited while in Chattanooga is part of this park.

The Battle of Chickamauga was a Confederate victory in September of 1863. It allowed southern troops to move north and besiege Chattanooga which Union forces had occupied earlier. The Battle of Lookout Mountain was part of the Battle for Chattanooga which broke the siege.

**Georgia Monument, Chickamauga Military Park (Dec 26, 2012)**

The road goes right by the visitor center which holds a nice museum with an impressive collection of guns. Georgia's monument is the largest in the park but there are many others, both large and small, and plenty of information panels.

Once it reaches Rome, the loop moves onto GA 293 and heads almost due east to reconnect with the DH West Mainline near Cass, Georgia. As planned, I put the Dixie Highway aside and drove the path of least resistance into Atlanta where I spent a couple of days seeing local sights. When I moved on, I headed east on the Dixie Highway Georgia Connector.

The connector begins near downtown Atlanta where US 29 separates from US 41. It follows US 29 east along North Avenue. Within a few blocks it passes the original Varsity. The Varsity opened in 1928 and is now the "World's Largest Drive-in". There are now several locations in the area but this is where it all started.

An eatery with even bigger reach started just a few miles further on after the connector moves onto US 278. The very first Waffle House still stands in Decatur, Georgia, although it has been converted to a museum. It is normally open only by appointment.

**Alcovy Road east of Covington, GA (Dec 28, 2012)**

City congestion eased up but the road stayed several lanes wide until near Lithonia where US 278 moves over to piggyback on I-20 and the DH Georgia Loop stays the course onto the two-lane Old Covington Highway. It wasn't instant peace and quiet but it was nice to have all those lanes and the majority of Atlanta traffic behind me. The road follows the railroad through some semi-open spaces then again hooks up with US 278 and some almost city traffic as it works its way through Covington. It leaves Covington on Alcovy Road which gets down to two lanes rather quickly and eventually even looks a little rustic in spots.

**Signed Dixie Highway east of Madison, GA (Dec 28, 2012)**

About half way through the twenty some mile drive to Madison, the connector enters Morgan after a brief encounter with US 278 and the name Dixie Highway starts to appear. It continues to be used into the city where it is replaced by Dixie Avenue.

At Madison, the connector turns south onto Eatonton Road which carries both US 129 and US 441. The two US routes split south of Eatonton with the connector following US 441 toward Milledgeville. The 1954 creation of Lake Sinclair submerged the original road near the halfway point between Eatonton and Milledgeville. I left the main road and drove down to the lake then returned to US 441 and crossed the lake to drive down to the shore on the other side, too. Clusters of houses and branching roads left me unsure whether I had actually followed the old Dixie to the water on either side. However, from the south edge I was able to reach and follow the old road, GA 212, into Milledgeville. Milledgeville is not a large city and I always have trouble picturing it as the capital of Georgia which it was until after the Civil War.

**G.R. Giles Grocery, Giles Corners, GA (Dec 29, 2012)**

The connector leaves Milledgeville on GA 24 then turns onto Deepstep Road a few miles east of town. The scenery on Deepstep includes O'Quinn's Mill, established in 1807, and G.R. Giles Grocery, established in 1922. The grocery store stands in one corner of the intersection that forms Giles Corners. All four have been owned by the Giles family since 1805.

The DH Georgia Connector moves onto GA 24 at Sandersville but remains picturesque two-lane right up to its end at US 25 in Waynesboro.

Now that I was keeping track of my Dixie Highway travels, I could see where I had yet to go. There was a whole bunch of yet to be driven DH in the south and a noticeable amount up in eastern Michigan. No surprise there, I thought, those are areas that take some effort to reach from Cincinnati. A third area that remained unmarked did surprise me. About 360 miles of the West Mainline, everything north of Louisville, Kentucky, was still tauntingly blue on my scoring map. What makes this so surprising is that Louisville is barely 100 miles from my home and Chicago, the other end of the undriven segment and the West Mainline terminus, barely 250. I often pass through or near Louisville on trips to the south but apparently had yet to approach from or depart to the northwest. I got a chance to change that in the spring of 2013.

The occasion was the premier of a film that a friend was involved in at the Nashville Film Festival. Before I left home, I made plans to fill that gap between Indianapolis and Louisville. I worked in some previously driven Dixie Highway on the way to the festival and encountered a super surprise.

It was September of 2010 when I'd last stopped at the Horse Shoe Camp Motel and it appeared doomed. It had been in a slow decline since my first sighting in 2004 and in 2010 a portion of the roof had collapsed. That slow decline seemed about to accelerate. I drove by it in the rain in December of 2011 but it looked the same and I didn't even bother to stop. I was dumbstruck by what I saw today.

**Horse Shoe Camp Motel near Bowling Green, KY (Apr 18, 2013)**

A new roof covered the office area and canopy and new plywood covered the windows and door opening. The rooftop sign that once appeared about to tumble into the breach was level and secure. I had no idea, of course, of what might have triggered the sudden change but I sure was pleased. Old motels with collapsing roofs are much more likely to be bulldozed than repaired. I was astounded. Oh happy day.

I enjoyed the southbound drive and a couple of nights in Nashville. Of course, enjoying nights and days in Nashville is pretty much a given. The film festival was great, the music, as always, fantastic, the food wonderful, and I even got to explore outside the city for a bit. When it came time to leave, I used the expressway to scurry to Louisville.

Expressways and other modern intrusions make it impossible to actually follow the Dixie Highway into Indiana. I picked it up on State Street in downtown New Albany. The DH merged onto the divided four-lane US 150 within a few miles but that four-lane didn't last long. The road narrowed within a mile. There would be other much longer stretches of divided four-lane on the way to Indianapolis but it would be pleasant countryside and small towns all the way.

Orange County courthouse, Paoli, IN (Apr 20, 2013)

One of those small towns is Paoli where the Dixie Highway leaves US 150 to follow IN 37 north. The change is made at the town square which has the 1847 Orange County courthouse sitting in its center. Not only does the courthouse look great, it is one of those rare historic buildings that can actually be photographed without a web of modern poles and cables intruding and blocking various bits.

**Old Indiana State Road 37, Cascade Park, Bloomington, IN (Apr 20, 2013)**

State Road 37 is the current incarnation of the DH in these parts but there are quite a few segments of the old road scattered along the way. Many carry the name Old State Road 37. One of these goes through downtown Bloomington. This was the closest thing to a city that I drove through before reaching Indianapolis but the minor congestion was more than compensated for when I followed the road through Cascade park at the north edge of town.

Indianapolis, of course, is a real city but that is where I ended the Dixie Highway portion of the trip. I spent the night there and did some exploring the next day but the DH portion of the trip ended when I reached the Soldiers and Sailors Monument whose column topping Victory I had last seen sitting at ground level just over a year and a half ago.

**Approaching Soldiers & Sailors Monument in Indianapolis, IN (Apr 20, 2013)**

In September, the Dixie Highway became a target of opportunity when I headed north for the bicentennial of the Battle of Lake Erie. Oliver Hazard Perry's victory over the British on September 10, 1813, was a real turning point in the seemingly almost forgotten War of 1812. I didn't firm up plans to go until it was too late to book a spot to see the planned reenactment but I did get to Put-In-Bay to see some of the tall ships gathered for the occasion.

I remained focused on the War of 1812 for a few more days as I drove into Canada to visit other sites associated with the war. These included the site of the Battle of the Thames where the Shawnee chief Tecumseh was killed in another British defeat about a month after their loss to Perry.

Entry to and exit from Canada was through Detroit which put me in a near perfect spot to drive two pieces of Dixie Highway when I returned to the States. I immediately headed to Cadillac square to pick up Gratiot Avenue and the southern end of the DH Port Huron Loop.

The first part of the drive was not pretty. Within a few blocks empty buildings and empty lots became the dominant features. Graffiti covered most of the empty buildings and a few were burned out. As I recall, I was nearly five miles from Cadillac Square before things started looking normal. This was near the bottom of Detroit's decline. The city had filed for bankruptcy less than two months earlier. It would exit bankruptcy by the end of 2014.

Of course, even normal looking cities aren't often scenic and the fact that much of Gratiot Avenue is divided six or more lanes didn't help. In Port Huron, however, I found something that made it all worthwhile.

Chicken in the Rough, Port Huron, MI (Sep 3, 2013)

There were once at least 250 Chicken in the Rough franchises. Now there are, according to the company's website, three. It all started in 1937 and peaked in the 1950s. Port Huron's Palms Krystal Bar and Grill is the only official franchise in the United States. The other two are across the border in Sarnia, Ontario, Canada.

I'd heard of Chicken in the Rough, of course, but thought I might never see one. I was overjoyed when a friend told me about this one and I had a chance to try the legendary meal. Sometimes big time anticipation can lead to real disappointment but not this time. Ever since I pulled out of the parking lot, I've been looking for an excuse to return.

**Bathing Beach Park, Harbor Beach, MI (Sep 3, 2013)**

The loop picks up the Michigan State Route 25 designation at the south edge of Port Huron and things are more scenic above the city as the road becomes two-lane and runs near the Lake Huron shore. The view of the lake is often blocked by trees or buildings, however. In Harbor Beach, I momentarily left the Dixie Highway to get a picture of the lake and pier at Bathing Beach Park. The white dot in the distance is the 1884 Harbor Beach Lighthouse.

At Harbor Beach, the loop moves onto State Route 142 and heads to Bad Axe. That's where I spent the night. I was sure there had to be a good story behind the name and asked the motel clerk. She warned me that I would be disappointed then explained that early surveyors found a broken axe here and had noted it on their map. I had indeed imagined something much better.

The loop continues on MI 142 until it ends at MI 25 just south of Bay Port. From there, it's MI 25 all the way to the Dixie Highway East Mainline at Bay City.

The Dixie Highway Flint Bypass Loop is one of those segments with no known Dixie Highway Association documentation. Setting it apart from other loops is that it is described as starting, not at one of the mainlines, but from the Port Huron Connector a little over two miles before it reaches the West Mainline in Bay City and is named not for a city it passes through but one it avoids. That last fact is, of course, reflected in the word "Bypass" in its name.

**Root beer float at the A&W in Ortonville, MI (Sep 4, 2013)**

Since I have found no official DHA information nor any other contemporary description of the route, it's possible that those oddities are merely modern day quirks. Having directions at hand, I drove the loop to be on the safe side. I saw no Dixie signage of any sort which makes its authenticity even more in doubt. As a result, I can't say with certainty that this root beer float was actually served on the Dixie Highway. It tasted as if it might be, though.

# 11 FITTING IN A FEW MILES

It was still summer of 2013 when a real craving for Key West, Florida, struck and I voiced my intention to spend Christmas there. I would certainly cover some Dixie Highway along the way. The intention still held after my September Canada and Michigan drive but as December approached, reasons not to do it started popping up. I put it off to January and then February. The arrival of March's warmer temperatures made me decide that next winter would be soon enough.

The Key West craving remained and it was now accompanied by the disappointment of missing the anticipated Dixie Highway miles. Apparently I was really starting to think in terms of finishing the whole thing and almost all of what I had remaining was in the south. In July, I included some Dixie Highway in a trip that began with no DH connection whatsoever.

Plans for the trip started percolating when I realized that I could combine a trip to a Route 66 festival in Kingman, Arizona, with a visit with my son in San Diego, California. With San Diego, in the mix, I began looking for a route to or from that city that included some new-to-me road. I ultimately decided on the Old Spanish Trail, a named auto trail that ran to San Diego from Saint Augustine, Florida. There is no doubt that the availability of undriven Dixie Highway between Cincinnati and Saint Augustine influenced my decision to some extent. I was very much aware of it when I started plotting my route.

A big chunk of the West Mainline, all the way from Chattanooga, Tennessee, to Punta Gorda, Florida, remained and I had sort of planned on someday doing that in one shot. I could not do it all this trip and did consider saving the stretch that I could do but decided not to wait. I started the Dixie Highway portion of the trip in Chattanooga and headed southeast. California, here I come.

**Bachman Tubes under Missionary Ridge, Chattanooga, TN (Jul 28, 2014)**

The 1916 Scarborough Tour Book indicates that the West Mainline and the Rome Loop both headed south through Rossville, Georgia. They split after reaching the Chickamauga Battlefield with the mainline turning east to Ringgold. I had problems sorting this out at the time and opted for a simpler and more modern version. US 41 adopted much of the Dixie Highway and that's what the driving instructions I had told me to follow out of Chattanooga. Today's US 41 utilizes the Bachman Tubes to get through Missionary Ridge and I assume it did so from the day in 1929 when the tubes were opened. The Dixie Highway Association disbanded in 1927 so the tubes could never have been part of the official Dixie Highway. However, I imagine a lot of people felt they were on the Dixie

Highway when they drove through these tunnels in the 1920s and 1930s so it's no sin if I did, too.

**Gem Theater, Calhoun, GA (Jul 28, 2014)**

**Main Street, Hampton, GA (Jul 28, 2014)**

There are some very pretty tree lined stretches of the Dixie Highway through northern Georgia but there are also some not so pretty stretches where the roadside is filled with fast food franchises and used car lots. There are also some attractive small towns.

In Calhoun, the restored 1927 Gem Theater makes the town look good and it is back to presenting movies, concerts, and other entertainment, too. A couple of miles north of Adairsville, a signed section of Old Dixie Highway pulls away from the current US 41 to pass through town.

The old road again pulls away more than forty miles north of Atlanta to pass through small towns such as Acworth, Kennesaw, and Marietta. There is certainly traffic to deal with in Atlanta but it could be worse as the Dixie rejoins US 41 and passes east of the heart of the city. Around twenty miles south it moves onto Old Highway 3 and into Hampton. Hampton is quite an attractive town with a Main Street lined with well maintained older buildings.

**Old Dixie Highway near Folkston, GA (Jul 29, 2014)**

At Barnesville, the Dixie Highway and US 41 turn east and make their way to Macon where they turn southwesterly. About a dozen miles south of Macon, the Dixie Highway Southern Connector splits off and heads directly south. Now it is the connector that follows

US 41 while the mainline moves onto GA 49. I moved onto the connector.

In Perry, the connector trades US 41 for US 341 which it follows to Hawkinsville and US 129. The connector uses a variety of roads, including US 1, to reach the DH East Mainline at Jacksonville. A couple of the side roads are signed Old Dixie Highway. One with the Old Dixie Highway name leaves US 1 more than seven miles north of Folkston and continues all the way into town. There is no chance the striped and edged asphalt with trees set well back from the edges will be confused with a 1920s roadway but the image is a common one for Georgia and one that I always associate with the state.

As soon as I reached the East Mainline, I headed directly to Saint Augustine and the terminus of the Old Spanish Trail. I spent a relaxing afternoon and evening there then set out on the OST in the morning. For several years, the Dixie Highway Association listed a connector between Jacksonville and Tallahassee although its route was precisely that of the Old Spanish Trail. Prior to the release of their final official map in 1923, the DHA removed this connector at the request of the Old Spanish Trail Association. I get to benefit from that long ago sharing by chalking up the DH North Florida Connector while driving the OST.

The connector generally follows US 90 and, although there are some short sections of divided four-lane, it is pleasant two-lane most of the way. About eight miles west of Greenville, it went beyond pleasant when I left US 90 for a county road. The Dixie Highway driving instructions that I had would have kept me on US 90 but there were reasons to believe that the Old Spanish Trail went this way. Since a goal of the current trip was to drive the OST, there was never a question of whether or not I should drive it. There was, however, room for a little doubt as to whether or not it was the DH. The story I'm sticking with is that it is DH because the DH and the OST were supposed to be one and the same. Besides that, it's a mighty pretty road.

**Basset Dairy Road near Monticello, FL (Jul 30, 2014)**

The trip was just starting but reaching the Dixie Highway West Mainline a few miles east of Tallahassee marked the end of the North Florida Connector and the end of that round of Dixie Highway collecting.

I did have contact with the Dixie Highway one more time before the next trip that added to my tally. I had heard the news and I had seen the pictures but I still needed to see it myself. In November, on the way home from a visit to Franklin, Tennessee, I made a point of driving that section of Dixie Highway just north of Bowling Green, Kentucky.

**Horse Shoe Camp Motel near Bowling Green, KY (Nov 17, 2014)**

On April 22, what is believed to have been a meth lab explosion triggered a fire at the motel in the very first picture in this book. I have tagged the start of my Dixie Highway exploration to the date in 2004 when I took that picture. With infrequent visits, I watched the Horse Shoe Camp Motel slowly deteriorate until on my most recent stop, just four days and a year before the fire, I had been surprised by a new roof over the canopy and office.

The fire reportedly started in the rear of the cabins and winds quickly pushed it forward toward the office area. It had taken the new roof over the office but had been extinguished just before reaching the canopy. The roof mounted metal sign that I had watched tilt more and more as the roof below it slowly collapsed now stood eerily square and straight on the only solid roof ridge in the whole place.

# 12 CLOSING IN

It was a year later than I'd planned but I did finally get to Key West. When I had considered it in 2013, I figured I'd catch a couple of Dixie Highway segments on the way but now I targeted them all. By "all", I mean all of the segments to my south that I had not yet driven. That meant a bunch of West Mainline and four connectors in Florida. By the time I left home, I'd added another goal to the trip.

Friends were spending Christmas in Savannah, Georgia, and stopping by seemed like just the thing to do. The Dixie Highway East Mainline runs through Savannah so that seemed like a good way to get there. But I'd already driven that segment so perhaps I should just hurry to Savannah along the quickest path. On the other hand, I had missed seeing six of the eight Robert E. Lee and Dixie Highway markers along that route. Maybe I ought to take another look. In the end, that is what I decided to do and seeing those other six markers became a mission.

With the first marker at the Tennessee-North Carolina line, Newport, Tennessee, seemed like a good place to pick up the route. From Cincinnati, Knoxville is always a convenient first night's stop and it is close enough to Newport to support an early start on finding those markers. It would also let me have dinner at Litton's, a favorite restaurant on Knoxville's north side, and check up on a certain airplane, too.

**Nickle Brothers service station, Powell, TN (Dec 23, 2014)**

Comparing the first picture of this chapter with the last picture of the previous chapter is jolting. One roadside icon is slowly being resurrected while another is destroyed in an instant.

**Mini-museum in Marshall, NC (Dec 24, 2014)**

I found the markers at the state line and at Hot Springs then stopped in Marshall where I'd stumbled across the first marker I'd ever seen back in 2008. I would visit all eight Carolina markers by the end of the day and all ten known markers by the end of the trip. Pictures of each are at the end of this chapter.

I know nothing about the Star Diner but I could see changes since my last visit. It is clearly an ongoing project. Perhaps it will turn into an active diner or museum some day.

Sander Motor Court, Weaverville, NC (Dec 23, 2014)

Even though this day was primarily for marker hunting, armed with new information I was able to spot a few other things as well. Sander Court is one of four classic motels at the south edge of Weaverville. Following his success in Corbin, Kentucky, Harlan Sanders, the Colonel, built a second motel north of Asheville in Weaverville in 1939. Initially quite successful, both it and the one in Corbin suffered greatly with the start of World War II and Sanders sold this one in 1942. Spacing on the sign seems to indicate that the lack of a second 'S' in the name is intentional but I don't know why.

Marker hunting resumed with the one in Asheville and continued to the border between the Carolinas with a final find in Greenville, South Carolina. I spent the night in Augusta, Georgia, then drove through a day of rain to a really cool Christmas Eve with friends in Savannah.

On Christmas Day, I moved onto Saint Augustine, Florida, where I celebrated the holiday with something of a walkabout with another friend. On the following day, I headed over to Hastings, Florida, and the first new-to-me Dixie Highway of the trip. Hastings is where the East Florida Connector splits from the East Mainline to head to Orlando.

**Citron Avenue, Crescent City, FL (Dec 26, 2014)**

The wide and modern US 17 carries the bulk of the connector although there are spots on older alignments that harken back to an earlier day. Near the north end, parts of the route around San Mateo and Crescent City fit this description and so does a segment near De Leon Springs. In Orlando suburb Winter Park, the connector passes through a nine-hole golf course on brick pavement.

When the Dixie Highway East Florida Connector reached the West Mainline in Orlando, I turned away and scooted through the city on expressways. I had driven this section of mainline in 2012 and my next target was the start of the Central Florida Connector in Kissimmee.

Not long after it clears the city, the connector moves onto US 192 and basically hangs with it all the way to Melbourne. That means that it is mostly divided four-lane and not particularly exciting. There is one notable exception.

**Lake Lizzie Drive west of Saint Cloud, FL (Dec 26, 2014)**

West of Saint Cloud, almost three miles of old Dixie Highway, now called Lake Lizzie Drive, can still be driven. It has been covered with modern asphalt at some point but it looks to be the original width which I'm guessing was nine feet. You might have to squint just a little bit but you can definitely get close to that illusion of driving in the 1920s here.

I spent the night in Melbourne and even did a little seaside driving on A1A but only a little. I soon found my way to I-95 for a dash to the keys. In Miami, I-95 ends and dumps onto US 1 which is also signed Dixie Highway. At that point, even the pretense of dashing that I tried to maintain into the Fort Lauderdale-Miami area vanished. Dashing and that level of traffic simply do not mix. I continued onto the Overseas Highway, spent a couple nights on Marathon Key, and drove into Key West for a day. On my return to the mainland, I once again utilized expressway and hurried to the east end of the DH South Florida Connector.

Florida is mostly flat which means roads are mostly level. Unless they are following the coast line or weaving around lakes, they're usually pretty straight, too. The East Florida Connector does not run along the coast and there is only one lake between West Palm Beach and Arcadia. It happens to be the biggest lake in the state but there's still just one. The East Florida Connector is essentially two arrow straight and billiard table flat lines that angle around Lake Okeechobee.

**Possible old Dixie Highway east of Arcadia, FL (Dec 31, 2014)**

I hold strongly to the belief that there is something interesting to be found in every community and along every road. I had one or two things in mind as I approached the end of the connector but I'll admit they weren't grade A interesting things. Finding points of interest on fifty-five miles of straight and flat road with few towns can be a challenge. Then, with about a half dozen miles of connector left, I noticed remnants of brick pavement exactly paralleling the current road to the north. Interesting, definitely. Dixie Highway, maybe. The narrow roadway is fragmented and nearer town what looks like a similarly dimensioned concrete road appears along the same path. By the time the city limits are reached, it has morphed into a normal city sidewalk.

I took another break from the Dixie after the end of the connector was reached. I drove up to Showtown USA, the Gibsonton bar I first visited on Christmas Eve 2008. I even briefly thought of watching the new year begin there but in the end spent a quiet New Year's Eve in my motel room. On New Year's Day, I checked out the classic car museum in Sarasota then followed the Tamiami Trail to Punta Gorda where I returned to the Dixie Highway on the second day of the year.

Punta Gorda is where I picked up the Dixie Highway while driving the Tamiami Trail in 2008. Now I left the Tamiami Trail and headed north on the Dixie Highway West Mainline. As parts of the Dixie Highway, the Tamiami Trail and the roughly twenty-five miles of road between Punta Gorda and Arcadia are inseparable. Without the Tamiami Trail, the DH West Mainline turned east at Arcadia and followed the route that I had driven into Arcadia two days earlier.

**Old Homeland Road near Homeland, FL (Jan 2, 2015)**

US 17 has basically picked up the job of the Dixie Highway between Punta Gorda and Winter Haven and it performs it with four-lane efficiency. North of Zolfo Spring, however, quite a bit of the old road can be driven. It is now nicely paved, of course, but still offers something of a peek into the past. With the exception of some city streets in Bartow, it is all two-lane from Homeland all the way to Winter Haven.

**Florida State Route 17 near Waverly, FL (Jan 4, 2015)**

I left the Dixie Highway one more time in Winter Haven to spend a couple of days with my uncle at Lake Alfred. On departure, I returned to Winter Haven to close out the undriven stretch of mainline at Haines City then turned south on the Scenic Highlands Connector. The northern end of the connector shares its path with the state designated Ridge Scenic Highway which runs along the Lake Wales Ridge. The road actually climbs and drops and curves now and then. I have included a photo of motorcyclists topping a hill. It is a fairly rare scene in Florida and it's not due to a scarcity of motorcycles.

The connector moves onto US 27 a few miles south of Frostproof but soon leaves it at Avon Park. Not long after passing Sebring International Raceway the connector joins US 98 and soon after that it becomes a more typical flat and straight Florida road. It ends when it reaches the South Florida Connector at Okeechobee.

**Sebring International Raceway, Sebring, FL (Jan 4, 2015)**

That was the fourth and final connector of the trip. My next target was Orlando and the stretch of West Mainline between there and Macon, Georgia. I probably could have worked out some express route to Orlando but that didn't interest me. Instead I basically went back up the Scenic Highlands Connector to Haines City and followed the West Mainline section I had driven in 2012 back to Orlando although I wasn't overly meticulous about it and I did take some short cuts.

I spent the night in Orlando then drove to the intersection of Orange and Colonial in the morning. That's the point where I started my mainline drive south in 2012 and where I'd reached the end of the East Florida Connector ten days before. As it heads northwest, the Dixie Highway loosely follows the US 441 corridor. The following is so loose that, before reaching Leesburg, the DH is hardly on the US highway at all. Instead, it is often on county roads and small town streets that are occasionally named Old Dixie Highway. Leesburg also sort of marks the end of the winding that both US 441 and the DH have done working their way through the cluster of lakes along Orlando's west side.

In Leesburg, I turned onto US 27 from Dixie Avenue then turned off after a few miles to follow another Dixie Avenue through Fruitland Park. Before getting out of town, I was back on US 27 which had been joined by US 441 and, with a few exceptions, that was the combination all the way to Ocala. The two US highways separate at Ocala and the Dixie splits off to go more or less between them. It does rejoin US 441 but takes off again, about ten miles south of Gainesville, to lead me through the best surprise of the day.

**Herlong Mansion Bed & Breakfast, Micanopy, FL (Jan 5, 2015)**

I didn't even know Micanopy existed although it has been around since 1821. That was two years after Spain ceded Florida to the United States and twenty-four years before it became a state itself. That 1821 date refers to official founding by United States of America folks. Settlements of some sort existed here long before that. Hernando De Soto found a Timucuan Indian village here in 1539. There is an awful lot of history in Micanopy and a lot of it can be learned at the town's museum which occupies an 1890 warehouse. Many other historic building serve as shops and restaurants. The Herlong Mansion started as a large two story farm house in 1845 and got turned into a mansion by a wealthy owner in 1910. It has been a bed and breakfast since 1980. Micanopy calls itself "The Town that Time Forgot" and it seems to have a pretty good case.

When US 27 headed west at Ocala, it was to hook up with US 41. Together, they meet up with US 441 and the Dixie Highway about twenty miles beyond Gainesville. Following the meeting, US 41 and US 441 head off together toward the north as US 27 and the Dixie Highway head northwest toward Branford. I have a little extra affection for Branford. Early in this book, I mentioned a trip that my great-grandparents took in 1920 that I tried to retrace in 2001. There is a large spring in Branford which my great-grandmother mentioned in her letters and which I stopped at in 2001.

**Flooded spring in Branford, FL (Jan 6, 2015)**

The spring is still there and in 2001 was being used as a very nice swimming hole by local teenagers. I say "very nice" because it was surrounded by a wooden deck and steps. That part was now even nicer with wooden railings and fancier steps. But the nearby Suwannee had flooded over the spring and covered the deck. Locals told me that, while it was not all that unusual for the river to flood, it was highly unusual for it to happen in the middle of winter. Previous floods had happened in the spring. Usually March or April. This, they said, was not normal.

With only a couple of exceptions, the route from Branford to Tallahassee follows US 27 and with no exceptions worth worrying about, it is pleasant two-lane all the way.

I know I overuse the word "pleasant" but it is the best word I can find to describe this sort of drive. There are no majestic mountains or shining seas but neither are there several lanes of noisy traffic demanding attention or endless rows of car lots and fast food joints cluttering the roadside. There are few entertaining twists or turns but neither are there brain numbing minutes of idling at traffic lights or ticking off empty miles under cruise control. Those without a little back-road love in their soul might call it boring. Pleasant just seems right to me.

**Old Saint Augustine Road near Tallahassee, FL (Jan 6, 2015)**

The final approach to Tallahassee is a few notches above pleasant. Roads lined by trees arching over the pavement are not terribly rare and are probably more common in Florida than elsewhere. I've seen plenty of them. That the length of the tree-made tunnel on Old Saint Augustine is longer than most certainly registered with me but what really set it apart were the signs. Yellow signs identify it as a "CANOPY ROAD" and urge drivers to take it "SLOW". I've since learned that Leon County has designated a total of eight Canopy Roads and that some are longer than Old Saint Augustine Road.

**Old capitol backed by new capitol, Tallahassee, FL (Jan 6, 2015)**

The northbound Dixie Highway approaches Florida's capitol straight on. Of course, travelers during the Dixie's heyday would not have had the tall tower to deal with in their view. It appeared in 1977. The 1845 capitol is now a museum with much of the building restored to its 1902 appearance.

Tallahassee is less than twenty miles from the Georgia border and less than a mile from that border is the only Robert E. Lee and Dixie Highway marker in Florida and one of only two outside the Carolinas. A stop at this one completed my personal scorecard for seeing all ten known markers. There is a full set of pictures at the end of this chapter.

In Georgia, I encountered other markers. The DH enters Georgia from the south by cutting through the southeast corner of Grady County. It enters Thomas County a little less than eight miles later. Thomasville, the county seat, is an attractive city with a beautiful 1858 courthouse right on the Dixie and a three century old oak tree just a block off the route. North of Thomasville, there is what looks like a miniature Washington Monument at the county line. Thomas Co. is marked on its sides so I assume Thomas County erected it.

**Marker at Thomas-Mitchell county line, Meigs, GA (Jan 7, 2015)**

**Marker at Mitchell-Dougherty county line near Albany, GA (Jan 7, 2015)**

At the north edge of the county, another Mitchell neighbor, Dougherty County, erected a welcome arch over the road.

South of Albany, Georgia, following the Dixie Highway is done on local roads that often parallel US 19. Between Albany and Americus it is on the divided four-lane of US 19 itself. At Americus, the DH moves onto GA 49 which it follows all the way to a few miles short of Macon. Less than a dozen miles from Americus, a surprise awaited. I was certainly aware of Andersonville Prison, the Civil War prison camp where nearly 13,000 Union soldiers died, but did not really know where it was. It was here.

The first prisoners arrived February 25, 1864. The first burial was on February 27. The prison site and cemetery are two of the three areas that make up today's National Historic site. The burying ground was designated a national cemetery on July 26, 1865 and it remains an active cemetery. There are monuments and some partial reconstructions where the prison once existed. The third part of the site is the National Prisoner of War Museum established in 1998.

National Prisoner of War Museum, Andersonville, GA (Jan 7, 2015)

Andersonville has a reputation of being the worst of the Civil War prison camps. Maybe so but, "Whether held in the North or South, a prisoner of war was more likely to die than a soldier in combat."

GA 49 is modern two-lane until just past Fort Valley where it joins something called Peach Parkway and spreads into divided four-lane. I would definitely call the two-lane portion pleasant and even the Peach Parkway goes through pleasant countryside. The spot where the Dixie Highway moves from GA 49 to GA 11 is the same as where the DH Southern Connector branches off toward Jacksonville. Since I had driven the Southern Connector in July, reaching this spot meant I had covered all the Dixie Highway I had targeted for this trip. I could jump on the nearby I-75 and scoot home if I wanted. I didn't want.

The temperature in Georgia was frightful. I had stepped out of my motel in Bryon into 15 degrees Fahrenheit. Back home in Cincinnati it was even worse. Minus 9 degrees and a little snow and ice to go with it. I was in no hurry to leap from the fridge to the freezer so I avoided the expressway and continued following the Dixie Highway West Mainline.

I saw some familiar stuff, of course, but I saw some new-to-me stuff, too. In Atlanta, I finally got to eat at The Varsity. It's actually on the DH Georgia Connecter but it is close enough to the West Mainline to slip it in. In Cartersville, Georgia, I checked out the restored Coca-Cola advertisement – the first one ever – on the side of the Young Brothers Pharmacy.

I finally left the Dixie Highway in Chattanooga and started home on the expressway. As I drove it occurred to me that I may never again have an opportunity to stop at all ten of those Robert E. Lee and Dixie Highway markers in one trip. Back in Ohio, just before going home, I drove by the marker near Franklin, Ohio, to complete the set. That ended the trip and photos of all the markers follow.

TN-NC Border

Hot Springs, NC

Marshall, NC

Asheville, NC

Fletcher, NC

Hendersonville, NC

**NC-SC Border**

**Greenville, SC**

**Bradfordville, FL**

**Franklin, OH**

# 13 BUT NO CIGAR

When I reached home following that year end Florida trip, I felt I was nearly done. Only the couple of hundred miles between Indianapolis and Chicago remained and I set about considering dates for the final drive. It had been more than ten years since my quest began but it seemed reasonable to believe I could wrap it up before the eleventh year was completely over. It only seemed that way briefly.

With wonderful timing, an online Dixie Highway group was launched just two days before I headed south in December. The group quickly established itself as a place where fans of the DH could share information and ask questions. Two weeks after my return from Florida, a group post brought two undriven-by-me segments to my attention. One was an alternate alignment that I had been vaguely aware of but had forgotten while the other was a true surprise. Both were unquestionably legitimate and both needed to be driven by me. By this time I had pretty much embraced the idea of finishing at the original beginning. All thoughts of a run to Chicago were shelved pending getting the two latecomers taken care of.

The one I had conveniently forgotten was the alternate Cincinnati to Lexington alignment that I've identified as the Falmouth Loop. It seems to be one of those temporarily endorsed routes that were awaiting a permanent designation when the Dixie Highway

Association ceased to be. Even if it had ultimately been dropped by the DHA, it had been officially recognized in 1921 and it deserved to be driven. Besides, it was really really close. Being really close meant that I could drive the hundred mile long loop with just a single day of good weather. When the temperature hit fifty, I hit the road.

**Railroad underpass south of Maurice, KY (Mar 9, 2015)**

There is nothing overly dramatic along the Falmouth Loop and I saw nothing that identified it as Dixie Highway. Both road and sky were dry and relatively clear on the day I made my drive but the fifty degree temperature was a rather new thing and plenty of snow remained along the road.

The other late addition to my agenda was also about a hundred miles in length but it was a lot farther away. Initially, the Dixie Highway Northern Connector in southwest Michigan turned east around Muskegon to pass through Grand Rapids and Kalamazoo. This was not the most direct path plus the move away from the lake shore was unusual. I speculated that there was no bridge over the Grand River when the connector was first defined and that the shorter route simply wasn't feasible. That seems not to be valid as I've since learned that automobiles were being routed across the river on a drawbridge in 1916. Whatever the reason, the early routing swung inland between Muskegon and Niles. In 1923, a somewhat straighter path was added that more closely followed the shore of Lake Michigan and passed through the town of Holland.

I mulled over how and when to cover this "new" loop and even considered combining it with a trip to the Chicago terminus but, in the end, combined it with a trip to Ann Arbor for the 2015 Lincoln Highway Association conference. I was not at all concerned with which direction I traveled the loop and the fact that I drove it north to south had more to do with convenience than anything. I drove to Muskegon, spent the night there, and headed south in the morning.

**Two-lane at last near South Haven, MI (Jun 21, 2015)**

The Holland Loop isn't very dramatic, either. For one thing, roughly the first half, to near South Haven, is now divided four-lane. Much of the tree lined two-lane that carried me on to Benton was quite pretty and I know I shouldn't complain but I knew that Lake Michigan was just beyond those trees and had this idea that I was missing out on gorgeous views of water stretching to the horizon. I finally stopped at a place called Hagar Park to curb my frustration. I soon discovered two things: 1) the lake was many feet below the road and those water-at-my-door views I'd been imagining just weren't there, and 2) it was so foggy on the lake that, even after I'd climbed down steps to stand beside it, I could see maybe a hundred yards of water at most. I climbed back up the steps and, frustrations well curbed, drove on.

**Old Tavern Inn, Sumnerville, MI (Jun 21, 2015)**

In Niles, I reconnected with the Northern Connector. I'd driven it in 2011 but had learned something else from that online group I mentioned. I now turned north to re-drive a few miles and patronize the oldest business in Michigan. Although it was probably called something else (New Tavern Inn?), the Old Tavern Inn had already been operating as a stage coach stop for two years when Michigan became a state in 1837. It sits on a corner that's been bypassed by a smoothing of MI 51.

# 14 FINALE FINALLY

Plans for driving the Indianapolis-Chicago segment came together at roughly the same time as those for checking off the Holland Loop in Michigan. An overnight visit to Indianapolis by the Greater Cincinnati Miata Club was just the ticket.

I had purchased a 2003 Miata more than a year before and had been a member of the club for nearly as long. During the summer, there seemed to be fun outings happening at least once a month but they never lined up with holes in my schedule. This one not only lined up with a hole, its location was perfect. It occurred shortly after the Michigan outing that put me in a position to make my Dixie clinching drive and its destination was the city where I wanted to start that drive.

And I do mean start. Unlike most Dixie Highway segments which I happily drove from whichever end happened to be nearest, I wanted to drive this one from south to north. It was a complete accident that it was one of the few undriven pieces when I started thinking about finishing things off but once I realized that, I wanted it to be the very last. When the Dixie Highway name was first used, it referred to a proposed Chicago-Miami connection. There was no question that Florida's sunshine was the attraction and Miami the destination. Chicago was the starting point. So, if the highway's starting segment was to be my finale, I wanted to make it a true "first shall be last" moment and finish at the segment's – and arguably the highway's – beginning.

When I headed north to that conference and planned pass of the Holland Loop, I had felt secure in the knowledge that not quite a month would pass before I would be on my way to drive the final piece of the Dixie Highway system. Then, just days before the planned departure, my knowledge became rather insecure.

While revisiting a very creditable website, I noticed that it identified a road running through Valdosta, Georgia, as Dixie Highway. It even stated that the Dixie Highway Association had "added" this route in 1924.

Uh-oh! If true, that meant that my planned drive to Chicago would not be the clinch I anticipated. The club outing to Indianapolis was firm but I could delay the Chicago drive until I could get to Georgia or I could go ahead with it and clinch the route in Georgia sometime in the future. Neither option was at all appealing.

The route in question was a popular one that early Florida bound travelers often followed south from Macon rather than sticking with the official Dixie Highway through either Tallahassee to the west or Jacksonville to the east. The wisdom of those travelers is supported by the fact that the route was substantially converted to US 41 which was, in turn, pretty much followed by I-75. Among the wise travelers deviating from the DH at Macon (even though I'm not sure they knew they were on it) were my great-grandparents on that 1920 trip I've mentioned a few times. That meant I had more or less driven it myself in 2001 and maybe I could count that to avoid scrapping either the rapidly approaching drive or my desire to finish at the beginning. As it turned out, none of those changes were necessary.

I contacted the author of the online article and we had a really nice email conversation. He told me that further research had shown that, although a group from Valdosta may have attended a 1924 DHA meeting to petition the association to add their city, the DHA took no action. It's quite possible that the delegation didn't even get to present their case since that seemed to happen fairly often, too.

This was certainly not the only place where local perception and practice differed from the DHA's official view. The Flint Bypass and Monroe Loop immediately come to mind. Although I did include both of those alignments in my drives, a pretty good case could definitely be made for omitting either or both. I decided I didn't need to change my plans now. Besides, if someone wanted to challenge me on the Valdosta route, I could proudly say that both my great-granddad and I had been there and done that.

On Sunday afternoon, when the other club members headed back to Cincinnati, I stayed in Indianapolis ready to hit the Dixie in the morning. My intended route was tweaked just a bit that evening. I met with several road fan friends for dinner and one of them shared some of his local Dixie Highway research with me. That let me include bits of the original DH alignment that I would have missed otherwise. Both this and the Valdosta story serve as reminders of just how imperfect my, or anyone's, knowledge of what existed a hundred years ago is.

**Indianapolis Motor Speedway on Dixie Highway (Jul 20, 2015)**

The pieces I almost missed, Waterway Boulevard and Cunningham Road, are connected by 16th Street. 16th Street and the Dixie Highway go right by the Indianapolis Motor Speedway. This is also where the Prest-O-Lite factory that made IMS founders Carl Fisher and James Allison extremely wealthy once stood. It seems reasonable to think that Fisher might have envisioned an endpoint for his "great highway from Indianapolis to Miami, Florida" right around here.

Even if you didn't know about Carl Fisher and his Indianapolis home base, your attention might still be drawn to the Indiana capital on a Dixie Highway map. Within the state's borders, the highway looks simple and businesslike. It's a cross centered on Indianapolis. The route west of the city is often called the "L" or "dogleg". After dropping straight south from Chicago, the West Mainline turned almost directly east to reach Indianapolis. In downtown, it turned south toward Louisville. The Northern Connector followed a fairly straight line from South Bend and the Midwest Connector was also pretty much a straight line to the east and Dayton, Ohio.

**Old State Road 34 east of Jamestown, IN (Jul 20, 2015)**

All but about five miles of the base of the dogleg are in Indiana. US 136 has absorbed most of the old route but several remnants of the old road still exist. Crawfordsville, home of Civil War general and Ben Hur author Lew Wallace, is near the midpoint. Remnants east of Crawfordsville include a dead-ended but drivable two and a half mile long section of Old State Road 34 between Lizton and Jamestown. On the east side of Big Raccoon Creek, a portion of a wonderful section of brick paved New Ross Road can still be driven.

**New Ross Road near Big Raccoon Creek in Indiana (Jul 20, 2015)**

About twenty miles west of Crawfordsville, the old road leaves US 136 or maybe it is other way around. At US 41, the two US highways join up for a while and US 136 then passes through downtown Veedersburg to the north. The Dixie Highway continues due west and Dixie Bee Road signs soon appear beside the road. The Dixie Bee Line was a named auto trail that connected Chicago with Nashville, Tennessee. Apparently this was one of the places where the Dixie Highway and the Dixie Bee Line shared the road.

**Coal Creek Bridge, State Street (Dixie Bee Rd), Veedersburg, IN (Jul 20, 2015)**

The DH rejoins US 136 at Covington, Indiana, and crosses into Illinois just a few miles beyond. After a few more miles, it turns north onto the vertical part of the 'L' in Danville.

**Jarling's Custard Cup, Danville, IL (Jul 20, 2015)**

Danville is a worthwhile stop with plenty of history and some nice public artwork. An ice cream stand at its northern edge has been serving cool goodness since 1949.

With that turn to the north, the Dixie Highway and US 136 join up with IL 1. When US 136 turns west, after about a dozen miles, the Dixie stays with IL 1 and the two travel together all the way to Chicago Heights.

**D.A.R. Dixie Highway Marker, Hoopeston, IL (Jul 20, 2015)**

In another dozen miles, McFerren park, in Hoopeston, appears on the east side of the road. Almost lost in the cluster of signs from fraternal and other organizations is one of the Dixie Highway's oldest surviving markers. The stone and plaque in the center of the photo were placed by the Daughters of the American Revolution in 1920. The plaque reads:

```
DIXIE HIGHWAY
THE ORIGINAL HUBBARD TRAIL
ERECTED BY
BARBARA STANDISH CHAPTER
DAUGHTERS AMERICAN REVOLUTION
HOOPESTON ILLINOIS
1920
```

The Hubbard Trail, which the Dixie Highway follows in this area, was blazed by Gurdon S. Hubbard in the early 1820s.

There is an even older marker associated with the Dixie Highway about eighty miles north. Those eighty miles include a number of towns, much open country, and some roadside attractions such as the 1931 Watseka Theater in Watseka, the 1926 Balmoral Park racetrack near Crete, and an 1835 Gurdon Hubbard Trail stone marker (unreadable but next to a very readable 1936 monument) in Crete.

Arche Fountain, Chicago Heights, IL (Jul 21, 2015)

The "older marker" is in Chicago Heights just south of where IL 1 and the Dixie Highway part company. It is a fountain erected by the Arche Women's club in 1916 to mark the intersection of the Lincoln Highway and the Dixie Highway. The photograph faces north with the Dixie Highway West Mainline heading off beyond the fountain.

The fountain includes a likeness of Abraham Lincoln and three Lincoln quotes. One is the "With malice towards none..." line from his second inaugural address that is also quoted beside the Dixie Highway in Cincinnati. The other two are from a speech he gave in Springfield, Illinois, at the age of 28. One of these, "We find ourselves in the peaceful possession of the fairest portion of the earth", is often mentioned in descriptions of the fountain. I'm guessing that people might think it refers to the area around the fountain. I know I thought that might be the case. Lincoln was actually referring to the entire United States when he made the speech but that doesn't necessarily mean that people weren't thinking more locally when they chose it for the fountain. I was not very surprised to learn that Lincoln wasn't thinking only of Illinois when he spoke of "the fairest portion of earth" but I was surprised to learn that the reason for the speech was the burning to death of a negro by a mob in Saint Louis and that its subject was "The Perpetuation of Our Political Institutions" which had, as he notes in the speech, been preserved "for more than fifty years". That's pretty heavy stuff for a guy in his twenties and the speech seems to hint at another, better known one, he would deliver in Pennsylvania when his age had nearly doubled.

When the DH veers away from IL 1, it is actually signed Dixie Highway and that continues for over eight miles until it crosses Sibley Boulevard and becomes Western Avenue. Near the midpoint of this stretch lies Homewood, a village that seems to have really embraced its Dixie Highway connection. Three of the village's many murals depict Dixie Highway scenes and a small park on the corner of Dixie Highway and Hickory Road contains a pair of informative DH related signs.

A few open spaces exist between the start of Western Avenue and downtown Chicago but not many and, as the building density increases, so does the traffic. It wasn't really horrible, though, on the Wednesday morning that I drove it. Ten-ish on a weekday might be an OK time to drive into the city center.

My final miles of Dixie Highway would be on Michigan Avenue. In theory, I should have picked it up at its 'T' with 63rd Street but it is now one-way southbound at that point. I drove about four miles of Indiana Avenue, its northbound counterpart, until they merged into a two-way Michigan Avenue.

I don't really know whether or not the Dixie Highway Association designated a specific intersection for the Chicago start/end point. Multiple guide books from the period begin their directions at Jackson Boulevard and Michigan Avenue. The online directions at us-highways.com start at Washington Street and Michigan Avenue and I've read of early official tours beginning there. I've also read of tours beginning at the Art Institute which might indicate Adams Street and Michigan Avenue.

**Possible DH terminus at Washington & Michigan, Chicago, IL (Jul 22, 2015)**

I chose to end my quest at Washington Street for a couple of reasons. The most important one being that it is the most northern of the candidates and reaching it would mean I had also driven through the others. The second reason was that it was very near the relatively new Millennium Park and the sculpture that has quickly become a Chicago icon. The park opened in 2004 and *Cloud Gate* was completed in 2006. There is no sign or any other photo worthy indication of the Dixie Highway terminus and The Bean, as the gleaming *Cloud Gate* is commonly known, became my own symbol for the highway's starting point and the completion of my mission.

I parked in an underground garage and walked to the park. I had glimpsed The Bean as I drove by and it was partially visible as I entered the park but I did not approach it until after I had visited several other Millennium Park attractions. I did eventually walk up to *Cloud Gate* and around and under it. The picture below was taken facing west with what was once the Dixie Highway passing between the sculpture and the skyscrapers. Only then did I return to the open air café at the edge of the park and celebrate my clinch with a pilsner from Chicago's Goose Island brewery. 5,786 miles for a beer and a Bean? Absolutely!

*Cloud Gate* near Dixie Highway terminus in Chicago, IL (Jul 22, 2015)

# 15 REFLECTIONS

Eleven years is a long time and a lot changed while I was rolling through those Dixie Highway miles. There are the obvious physical things, like the fall, rise, and fall of the Horse Shoe Camp Motel and the continuing rise of the Nickle brothers' airplane shaped service station, but the change that is most significant to me personally is not physical although it might be obvious. I'm referring to the change in my own perception of the Dixie Highway and my recognition of its uniqueness. From originally thinking it a simple A to B highway, I moved to a feeling that it was a haphazard collection of paths that included every little chunk of road that someone suggested before finally seeing that it really was a system with an organization behind it trying to maintain standards in both quality and routing.

The modern high-speed cruise-controlled air-conditioned expressway-embracing version might have little in common with the originals but the Dixie Highway played a big part in the creation of snowbirds. Snowbirds are people, usually retired, who live in the north but head south with the approach of winter and snow. They can now be found in Arizona, Texas, and all other sunbelt states but the oldest flocks are in Florida and, like my great-grandparents, many of the first generation made their way south at least partially on the Dixie Highway. And they also went home on it.

The round-trip nature of many early Dixie Highway trips is different from most contemporary long distance drives on other named auto trails. Doing it multiple times was also a difference and was what gave rise to the name "snowbird". Unless your name was Joy, Hoag, or Ostermann, you probably did not drive the entire Lincoln Highway more than once and the odds were high that it was a one-way drive with return via train. Even Joy and company were known to ride the rails home now and then. Miami and Tampa were closer to Michigan and Indiana, where the cars were, than San Francisco or Los Angeles and I'm guessing that a lot more of those cars returned from Florida than ever came back from California.

**A happy me reflected in The Bean at journey's end (Jul 22, 2015)**

Of course that change in perception I mentioned was a direct result of my increasing knowledge. I don't think I've ever returned from a road trip without soon learning of something I missed. That has been particularly true of Dixie Highway trips. It might be surviving bits of road that I was unaware of or roadside attractions or scenic views that I just didn't notice. I have already repeated some sections and corrected some oversights but I almost certainly missed some things on my second and third passes, too. Big and complex and often confusing, the Dixie Highway is ripe for exploring.

# ABOUT THE AUTHOR

Denny Gibson is a retired software engineer living on the outskirts of Cincinnati, Ohio. He is addicted to driving two-lane highways and, since 1999, has documented his travels on them at DennyGibson.com. His photographs and writings have appeared in other travel books and magazines. He is the author of *By Mopar to the Golden Gate* which tells the story of driving the Lincoln Highway during its centennial year in a fifty year old car.

www.ingramcontent.com/pod-product-compliance
Lightning Source LLC
Chambersburg PA
CBHW061827040426
42447CB00012B/2845